Save the Scraps
Great Quilts from Small Bits

GAYLE BONG

Martingale®
& C O M P A N Y

Save the Scraps: Great Quilts from Small Bits
© 2005 by Gayle Bong

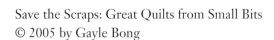

That Patchwork Place® is an imprint of
Martingale & Company®.

Martingale & Company
20205 144th Avenue NE
Woodinville, WA 98072-8478 USA
www.martingale-pub.com

Credits

President: Nancy J. Martin
CEO: Daniel J. Martin
VP and General Manager: Tom Wierzbicki
Publisher: Jane Hamada
Editorial Director: Mary V. Green
Managing Editor: Tina Cook
Technical Editor: Erana Bumbardatore
Copy Editor: Sheila Chapman Ryan
Design Director: Stan Green
Illustrator: Robin Strobel
Cover and Text Designer: Stan Green
Photographer: Brent Kane

Printed in China
10 09 08 07 06 05   8 7 6 5 4 3 2 1

Library of Congress
Cataloging-in-Publication Data

Bong, Gayle.
    Save the scraps : great quilts from small bits
/ Gayle Bong.
        p. cm.
    ISBN 1-56477-599-2
  1. Patchwork—Patterns. 2. Quilting.
3. Patchwork quilts. I. Title.
    TT835.B622 2005
    746.46'041—dc22
                                    2005003484

Mission Statement

Dedicated to providing quality products
and service to inspire creativity.

contents

introduction

AS YOU MIGHT IMAGINE, after 20 years of prolific quiltmaking, I've acquired a sizable collection of fabric. Now imagine the sheer volume of my scraps, considering that I've always had a hard time throwing away so much as a two-inch square when I knew that it could be used in a fantastic quilt someday!

Well, the time finally came for me to use these saved scraps, and do you know what? It turns out that I love scrap quilts best of all. Most quilters do, I think. Scrap quilts seem to be the universal favorite. They fit easily into today's casual lifestyle, and multifabric scrap quilts blend more easily into any decorating scheme than quilts with strict color and design schemes do. Best of all, they are more fun to make because of the variety of fabric they include.

I joined the quilting revolution at the time the rotary cutter was introduced. This time-saving tool quickly became every quilter's favorite new gadget, and we were all eager to see just how quickly we could cut out a whole quilt with it. A quilt with three or four different fabrics could be cut more quickly than a quilt with 25 or 50 fabrics, of course, so we tended to make lots of four-fabric quilts. Four-fabric quilts are still a joy to make using strip-piecing techniques, but now we want to slow down and enjoy combining the colors, patterns, and textures of the many prints and colors in our bulging scrap bags. Of course, we still use the rotary cutter and strip-piecing techniques we've come to love—they can't be beat for fun and accuracy.

Whether your scraps are organized neatly, a tangled mess of leftover patches and strips, or a growing collection of fat quarters, my favorite scrap-quilt designs, gathered in this book, will work for you. Before we jump right into the projects, though, I'll give you a few suggestions for getting your scraps organized and for choosing fabrics for successful scrap quilts. Then we'll cover some general quiltmaking techniques, followed by patterns for 15 great scrap quilts.

Quilters of all skill levels will enjoy the wide variety of techniques this collection of patterns offers. You'll use general strip piecing, folded corners, trimming to shape after sewing, sandwich piecing, Mary's Triangles, and split diamonds. You don't need to learn all the ins and outs of the technique used in the quilt you're making. Just choose your pattern, follow it, and know that you'll have fun and learn as you go!

I hope some of my quilts inspire you to use your long-hoarded scraps. Take a few minutes to look through the patterns and decide whether you want to try the quilts with techniques that are new to you or if you want to stay in your comfort zone and sew to your heart's content. May you enjoy your quilts many times over as they warm your heart and home.

organizing scraps

MANY LONGTIME QUILTERS have a system for dealing with the scraps that accumulate from sewing so many quilts. I applaud those quilters, unless their idea is to toss the scraps in the "circular file"! My casual polls at guild meetings across the country indicate that most of us save our scraps. But do you use them? Would you use them more if they were organized?

Over the years I made a few attempts at organizing my scraps before I found a system that truly worked for me. I really enjoy sorting and organizing fabrics, and I sometimes fantasize about starting a service where I would go from house to house organizing other quilters' stashes. Knowing this isn't likely to happen (how many people would actually hire me to come to their houses and play with their fabrics?), I'll tell you what works for me and give you some additional suggestions in case my way just doesn't work for you. There's something here for any quilter who believes that she would be more likely to use her scraps if they were organized.

At one time I kept my fabric in a four-drawer dresser, but I only had enough fabric to fill the top three drawers. As I worked, I would toss my scraps very carelessly into the bottom drawer. Eventually the drawer became stuffed with tangled strips and leftover bits and pieces of my latest masterpieces. Now I have a different system, and the most that gets out of hand is a medium-sized basket I keep on my cutting table specifically for scraps. Once the basket is full (or usually overflowing), I sort the scraps into my main scrap stash (described below). How you sort your scraps will depend on how many you have. Starting when your collection is small will certainly make the job easier.

If you have a small collection, you can consider sorting your scraps into two bins, one for light colors and one for dark colors. If you have a larger collection, such as the drawer full of scraps that I had, you may need more than two bins. I wasn't sorting long before I realized that most of my scraps were actually strips of varying widths and lengths. Therefore, another option is to separate the strips from the rest of your scrap pieces rather than separating the dark colors from the light colors. When the box of strips starts to bulge, you can begin a scrap quilt like "Fractured Diamonds" (see page 80).

One box for strips and one for other pieces doesn't take up much room, but if you have the space, perhaps combining the suggestions above would work for you. Try four boxes: light strips, dark strips, light pieces, and dark pieces.

Another logical breakdown for even larger scrap collections would be to sort by color. Color categories can be general or specific. Sort by warm colors, cool colors, and neutrals, or have a bin for each of the primary, secondary, and neutral colors. Sorting scraps by color might be a good choice if you like to make scrap quilts that follow a color recipe—quilts where specific colors are assigned to particular patches or positions in each block. I personally never sorted my scraps by color. I skipped that option and went straight to sorting by size.

My scrap stash fills a good portion of my closet. The strips are all sorted by width (1¼", 1½", 1¾", 2", 2¼", 2½", 3", 3½", and 4½"), and each width has its own *labeled* box on the closet shelf. The scrap squares and triangles are boxed and ready to use, too. I have boxes for 2", 3", and 4" finished squares and also for half-square triangles. The smallest pieces from my tabletop scrap basket can be cut to fill these boxes. The general rule of thumb is to cut the largest pieces you can from each scrap.

Mixed pieces of various sizes are in a boot-sized shoe box. This box includes units left over from other projects. I save these, and when the mood strikes I play with them, cutting other pieces to go with them to make a new block. They may not go with anything else, but they look good in the sampler quilts that I make and donate to a battered-women's shelter.

And finally, there are the "chunks" I keep in a small dresser drawer. Chunks are about ⅛-yard pieces of any shape. When the drawer gets full, I cut some of the chunks down to varying strip widths and file them. Cutting a variety of sizes ensures variety in my quilts.

Storage considerations may not be important in the grand scheme of things, but once your scraps are sorted, why not go one step further and arrange for storing them in an appropriate manner? You have to find what works best for you based on the size of your stash, the space available, and your budget. A single box on a shelf above your cutting table or in a closet may be all you need. But if you have a larger scrap collection, you will have to consider other options.

Perhaps you can store your scraps in an empty drawer fit with dividers or cardboard boxes cut to size. Boot-sized shoe boxes are my favorites. Plastic bins, boxes, and baskets are all good, too, provided they aren't too big. The bigger they are, the heavier they are, and the harder they are to go through to find what you need. This leads to wrinkles and tangling and may make you want to avoid your scraps altogether! If you only have space for one big box or tub, consider keeping your scraps sorted into clear bags inside the box.

START WITH A PLAN

Sorting your scraps is just the beginning—remember that sewing a great scrap quilt (or quilts!) is the ultimate goal. Here are some tips to help make sure you spend more time sewing than you do sorting.

- Plan two or three quilts before you begin to organize the scraps, and then cut and sort the scraps for those quilts right into their respective piles.

- Start a charm quilt, one where every patch in the quilt is cut from a different fabric. Every time you sort your scraps, set aside one same-sized scrap of each fabric you use.

- Allow a limited amount of space for your scraps. Tell yourself that once the allotted space is filled, you must use the scraps.

- Once your scraps are in order, make a rule that you must use scraps in your next quilt.

choosing fabrics

I HOPE THAT SORTING all your scraps inspires you to use them, but there's more to do before you're ready to start cutting out a quilt. Although choosing fabrics for a scrap quilt is probably easier than for other quilts, that doesn't mean you should adopt the "anything goes" theory.

Carefully choosing fabrics is just as important to the success of a scrap quilt as it is to any other. Begin by answering these two questions: **First,** what colors do you want your quilt to be? And **second,** what character or style do you want your quilt to have?

Color

The term *scrap quilt* suggests that in such a quilt, many prints are used in small doses. If that were the only rule, though, chaos would result. The fabrics in a scrap quilt should relate to each other. You can help make them relate by repeating colors in the scraps.

Consider these options to help you choose which colors to use in your quilt:

- Use the coordinating scraps you have the most of

- Use colors to coordinate with a specific room

- Use the quilt recipient's favorite colors

- Choose the colors that are in a favorite multicolored print

- Choose color harmonies that are your favorites

Pick the color or colors you want to work with, and don't try to make your scrap quilts look exactly like the quilts pictured in this book. The colors given in the patterns are just for reference to the color photographs.

Once you've decided on a color scheme and you're choosing fabrics, don't fret over whether everything matches perfectly. In the end, it's not too important if that little flower is orange and not pink, as long as all the fabrics "read" the same from a distance. It's a good idea to step back 10 feet from the fabrics you've picked to make sure they read as having the same tone, which will give your quilt a coordinated look. Different colors may all read as having a clear bright hue, a muted gray tone, a golden cast, or a brownish tinge. As long as the fabrics read the same, they'll work in your quilt.

Character

Here's the secret to a well-coordinated multi-colored scrap quilt: all colors work together if they relate to each other in character or style. You'll only create chaos if you mix too many different styles of prints. The style or character of a fabric describes the fabric's theme, such as reproduction prints, country style, contemporary, juvenile, holiday, ethnic, or novelty prints. All of these styles have their own sections in a quilt shop, and they should also have their own quilts. Most of your fabric stash may already coordinate in character. But if you enjoy making a variety of quilt styles, such as batik quilts, baby quilts, and folk art quilts, you will want to be choosy about which scraps you use together. Some prints blend easily with a variety of styles, while others are very specific and can be difficult to use in a scrap quilt. Set these scraps aside

These fabrics evoke a romantic mood.

These fabrics display vibrant energy.

until more of that style have accumulated, or choose a pattern that uses just a few scraps and then have them set the theme for the quilt.

Within the style you've chosen, plan to add variety by using prints with differing motifs. For the most interesting results, include flowers, geometrics, leaves, vines, swirls, dots, stripes, and so on, in all different sizes.

You can tweak your fabric choices even further to create a mood or feeling. Think of the fabrics that would define a romantic, sophisticated, quiet, subtle, and restful quilt. Both color and style of print could be used to define such a quilt. I picture soft pastels, low-contrast florals, and tone-on-tone prints. On the other hand, if I wanted a vibrant, intense, loud, lively, spirited, exuberant, or crisp quilt, I'd choose a busy quilt design, and I'd probably use high-contrast, zany geometric, or abstract prints in bright colors. So when you choose your fabrics, think about the mood you want to convey. In other words, do you want your baby quilt made of soft, sweet, innocent pastels or colorful, playful brights?

As you gather your prints, keep in mind that the more prints you incorporate into your quilt, the better, especially in a scrap quilt. In fact, the scrap quilt category in quilt shows often requires a minimum of 25 different fabrics. It is usually easier to use more fabrics because there are more of them to blend together. Any questionable fabrics will get lost in the mix. If a fabric stands out, you need to decide whether it clashes or is the spark the quilt needs. The piece that clashes frequently does so because it is out of character with the other fabrics.

Study the pictures of the quilts in this book and imagine them made with different colors and characters. Wouldn't "Another Mosaic" on page 58 look great in 1930s reproduction prints? And can you imagine "Full House" on page 50 in batiks and hand-dyed fabrics? What if "Good Neighbors" on page 30 were done in dark and medium prints, like "Geese in the Garden" on page 45, instead of two different colors? And I know "Fractured Diamonds" on page 80 looks great in a multicolored palette. The idea is for you to use the colors and character you like and not to feel limited by what I chose to use.

Contrast

In addition to color and character, you also need to consider the degree of lightness or darkness of a color. This is often referred to as a color's value. Fabric requirements for scrap patterns are often listed only as light or dark and not by color. Whenever a pattern calls for light, medium, or dark fabrics, it is important that you follow the directions carefully. If you don't, your quilt will not look the way you expect it to, because contrast is what makes the design. So, be sure there is enough contrast between the fabrics you've chosen for your scrap quilt.

Large-scale, high-contrast prints can be some of the most difficult fabrics to work with. When they are cut up into small pieces, it is difficult to classify them as light or dark because a single piece may have both light and dark sections. When the value of the fabric is mixed, the required contrast isn't there and the overall quilt pattern is lost to the eye. Some people like the fact that this makes your eye linger longer on the quilt by adding interest, and that's OK. But generally, I follow the rule that if you have to squint to see the block pattern, then there's not enough contrast from patch to patch, or there's too much contrast in the actual fabric prints.

Large-scale or high-contrast prints can still be used successfully if you follow one of these approaches:

- Blend many multicolored prints with similar colors and styles together

- Use equally busy, high-contrast prints throughout the quilt

- Use high-contrast prints in designs that let you isolate the print by surrounding it with solids (or other prints that read as solids) to create a distinct edge for each patch

As a quilt progresses, I like to put the blocks on a design wall and see if I need to tweak my

This large-scale print features colors with high contrast.

fabric selections. I might want the quilt to be more blue. Or maybe I think a certain red hue will add the sparkle the quilt needs, or that a medium shade blends into the background too much. Some prints don't work as well as I would have liked, so I replace the remaining pieces of that fabric. If I find I don't like one of the fabrics I've used, I don't hesitate to replace the offending patch or block. After all, the seam ripper is my friend—using it is part of the process of making a quilt I'll be happy with, and tearing out and replacing a patch takes just a few minutes.

I don't sew the darkest lights next to the lightest darks to avoid losing the pattern due to low contrast. When I get down to the last 8 or 10 pieces to sew together, I pair them up before sewing. This way I avoid unattractive combinations or using the same fabrics too close to each other. Eventually they will all be sewn together and I'll love it!

quiltmaking techniques and equipment

UNDERSTANDING BASIC QUILTMAKING TECHNIQUES and knowing how to use your equipment will make your quiltmaking more efficient and enjoyable. You don't have to master every skill discussed here before you start, though. If a pattern requires you to use a technique beyond basic rotary cutting and piecing, it will refer you back to this section.

Basic Rotary Cutting

The invention of the rotary cutter has allowed quilters to make quilts faster and with greater accuracy than ever before. If you're not already a rotary-cutting devotee, this section will tell you everything you need to know to master this fun and important skill.

Note: *If you are left-handed, you will need to reverse the fabric and cutting positions from what is shown in this section and throughout the project directions.*

Cutting Equipment

You'll need a few basic rotary-cutting tools to get started: a 24" straight-edged ruler for cutting strips, a rotary cutter, and a mat. Beyond these basics, a variety of rotary-cutting rulers are available and designed to cut specific shapes. A small square ruler is handy for crosscutting strips into individual pieces. Also recommended is a 45–90° triangle ruler designed for cutting 6" (or smaller) half-square triangles. This is a common specialty ruler that you you might already own. It could be the 6" Easy Angle, the Omnigrid 96, or maybe the Quilters Rule QRT-6. These tools allow you to cut triangles that include seam allowances.

Several of the designs in this book have 60° angles, and the directions for cutting these quilts specifically call for the Clearview Triangle Ruler. (See "Working with 60° Angles" on page 13.)

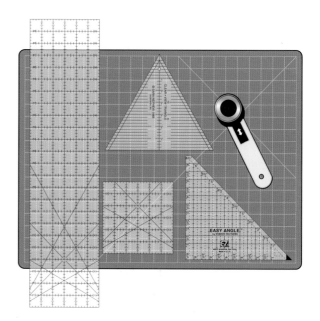

Squaring Up the Fabric and Cutting Strips

Before cutting strips, it's important to straighten the edge of the fabric. Strips are always cut first and then crosscut into the required size or set aside for strip piecing.

1. Fold the fabric in half lengthwise with selvages together, just as it comes off the bolt. If the fabric wrinkles along the fold, move

the top layer of fabric to the right or left to eliminate the wrinkles. Place the fabric on the mat with the fold closest to you.

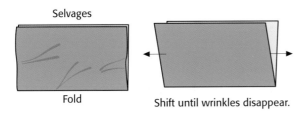

Selvages

Fold

Shift until wrinkles disappear.

2. Align a square ruler along the folded edge of the fabric near the edge you'll square up. This step is important; it will prevent you from cutting crooked strips as you make cuts perpendicular to the fold.

3. Push a larger ruler against the small one, remove the smaller ruler, and cut along the long edge of the larger one to square up the fabric.

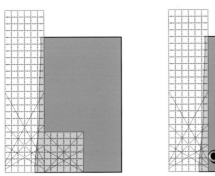

4. Without disturbing the fabric edges, fold the fabric in half again by bringing the fold up to the selvages, matching the just-cut edges. (A shorter cut makes the ruler easier to control.) The fabric is now in position to cut the strips. Center the line of the ruler with the correct measurement over the cut edge of the fabric. Cut along the edge of the ruler as shown.

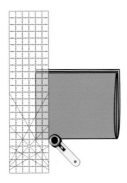

Cutting Pieces

Cut the number of strips required (as listed in the cutting chart for your project) or choose the correct-sized strips from your scrap stash. Place the strips crosswise on your mat, folded only once. Square up the ends to remove the selvages before crosscutting the strips. To trim the selvages, I usually cut the first piece larger than necessary, rotate it, remeasure, and trim off the selvage. (The measurements given in the patterns already include ¼" seam allowances.)

Cut **squares** the same dimension as the strip width.

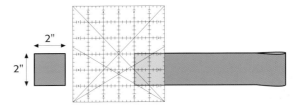

2"

2"

To cut **rectangles**, first refer to the cutting chart for your project. Sometimes the strip width will be the length of the rectangle and crosscuts will be the width of the rectangle, rather than the other way around.

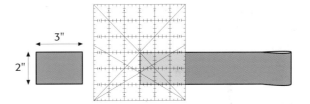

3"

2"

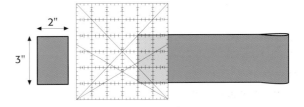

2"

3"

To cut **half-square triangles**, first cut squares the size specified in the cutting chart; then cut each square in half diagonally to create two half-square triangles. (The threads will run parallel to the short edges of the triangles.) Cut the diagonals immediately after cutting the squares. If you set aside the squares to be cut diagonally later, the layers are likely to shift and your cutting will be inaccurate.

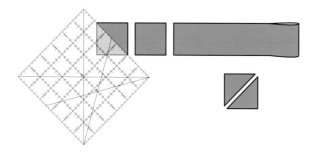

To cut **quarter-square triangles**, first cut squares the size specified in the cutting chart; then cut each square diagonally in both directions to create four triangles. (The threads will run parallel to the long edge of each triangle.) As with half-square triangles, cutting these diagonals right away will make your cutting more accurate.

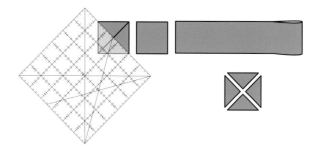

To cut and sew **equilateral triangles**, see "Working with 60° Angles" on the opposite page.

FOOLPROOF CUTTING

The following suggestions will help you achieve the most accurately cut pieces, whether you're cutting from scraps or yardage.

- Cut in daylight when possible, to avoid glare from overhead lights.

- Place the printed side of the ruler against the fabric. This helps to minimize misalignment of ruled lines.

- To keep the ruler from slipping while you cut, apply self-adhesive felt disks on the underside of the ruler.

- Always align the ruler lengthwise *and* crosswise with the piece you are cutting.

- Periodically straighten the edge of the fabric with a squaring cut, keeping it perpendicular to the fold, for strips that don't "bend" at the fold. This is especially important when the strips are being used for strip piecing or in borders.

- Remember a favorite tip of mine from the wood shop: check your pattern twice, check your ruler alignment twice, and cut once.

- Make your cut, and with the ruler still in place, slide the remaining fabric aside just a bit. You can see instantly whether you've cut through all the layers, and you won't need to reposition the ruler to complete the cut. You will also see if your rotary cutter wobbled away from the ruler. If it has, you will need to straighten each edge before continuing.

Working with 60° Angles

Three of the designs I have included in this book use equilateral (60°) triangles and related pieces. Many of our favorite quick-piecing techniques are adaptable to equilateral-triangle patchwork. There are several 60°-triangle rulers on the market, but they are each marked differently and may not all work with the patterns in this book. These patterns were written specifically for the Clearview Triangle Ruler, designed by Sara Nephew. The Clearview is made in several sizes; the 8" is my favorite.

In 60°-triangle patchwork, the finished size of the triangle is determined by measuring the height of the triangle rather than the length of its side. This applies to all pieces that are composed of equilateral triangles, including diamonds, parallelograms, and half triangles—the finished size of each of these pieces can be determined by the height of the piece. These pieces are cut from strips just like other patchwork. See top right.

Note: *If you are left-handed, you will need to reverse the fabric and cutting positions from what is shown in this section.*

Cutting

To cut **equilateral triangles,** place the triangle ruler on the strip at the end opposite the fold. Match the ruled line for the correct-sized triangle with the lower edge of the strip. The point of the ruler will meet the upper edge of the strip. Cut on each side of the triangle ruler to make your first triangle. For the next triangle, position the ruled line for the correct-sized triangle on the angled cut. Cut on the right side of the ruler. Alternate the position of the ruler for each triangle, always cutting on the right side of the ruler. See bottom right.

TIP As long as the strip width is correct and the point of the ruler does not extend beyond the top edge of the strip, your pieces should be the correct size.

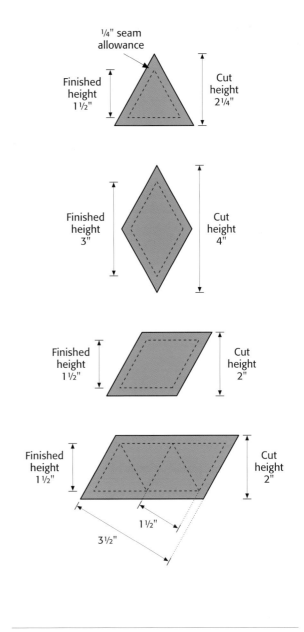

¼" seam allowance

Finished height 1½" · Cut height 2¼"

Finished height 3" · Cut height 4"

Finished height 1½" · Cut height 2"

Finished height 1½" · Cut height 2"

1½"

3½"

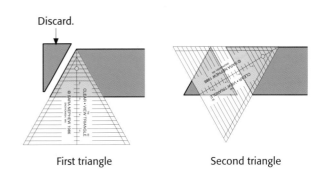

Discard.

First triangle

Second triangle

To cut **diamonds**, tip the triangle ruler to the left and use its lower edge to measure and cut a diamond the same length as the width of the strip. When you cut the first diamond, cut it extra large to allow for cutting off the selvage end. Rotate and trim the piece to the correct size.

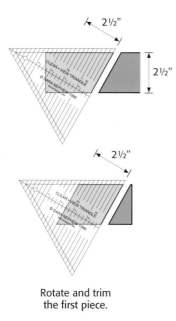

Rotate and trim
the first piece.

Continue to cut, using the ruled lines and measuring from the lower edge of the ruler. I like to place the ¼" line of the triangle ruler along the top edge of the fabric. This ensures accurate cuts because it is easier to see the fabric edge along the printed line than it is along the edge of the ruler. It does not affect the measurements of the piece being cut.

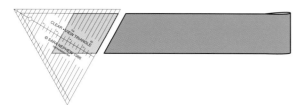

Parallelograms are cut like diamonds, with two exceptions. The first is that they are longer than the width of the strip, so be sure to follow the rule of checking your measurement twice before you cut. The second exception is that you cannot cut multiple parallelograms at one time. Always open the strip and cut a single layer of fabric. Otherwise a mirror image will be cut that can't be used in the pattern.

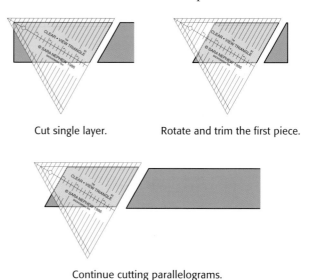

Cut single layer.   Rotate and trim the first piece.

Continue cutting parallelograms.

Half triangles are used at the edges of a quilt to square it up. They also have a mirror image. Half triangles are easy to cut from rectangles. To bisect the rectangles, place them wrong sides together and cut diagonally using a straight-edged ruler. Use a Clearview ruler in the corner to establish the proper angle.

Additionally, there are two strip-piecing techniques that let you cut already-sewn units. These are the three-patch triangle unit and split diamonds. These techniques are easier and more accurate than the traditional way of piecing these units, which is to cut and sew individual patches. Just like other strip-piecing methods, these techniques will have you sew some pieces together before cutting the unit to the correct size and shape. For details, see "Potluck" on page 75 and "Shimmer and Shine" on page 90.

3-patch triangle unit   Split diamond

Sewing 60°-Triangle Patchwork

For accurate 60° patchwork, it is very important that you correctly align your pieces before sewing. When the pieces are lined up correctly, they will form ¼" triangle extensions, often called mouse ears. Begin sewing at the end of the seam with this little ¼" triangle. (Do not trim these little triangles. They make great notches for matching up seams.) Use the full-sized illustration below as a guide for aligning the pieces correctly for sewing.

In 60°-triangle patchwork, each piece naturally has at least two bias edges. Be very careful not to stretch the fabric as you work with it. As you sew the smaller units together, just finger-press the seams before crossing each piece with other seams. As the units become larger and more complex, use the iron.

Strip Piecing

Most of the patterns in this book include strip piecing to speed production and increase the accuracy of the piecework. Strip piecing is a fun way to get the sewing done quickly without having to handle each piece individually. Cut, sew together, and press the strips as instructed in each project. Use the seam lines as a horizontal guide for the ruler when you square up the end of your strip set to trim the selvage ends. Then cut the strip sets into segments of the proper width to make the strip-pieced unit, again using the horizontal seam lines as guides. The units shown on page 16 are made in the

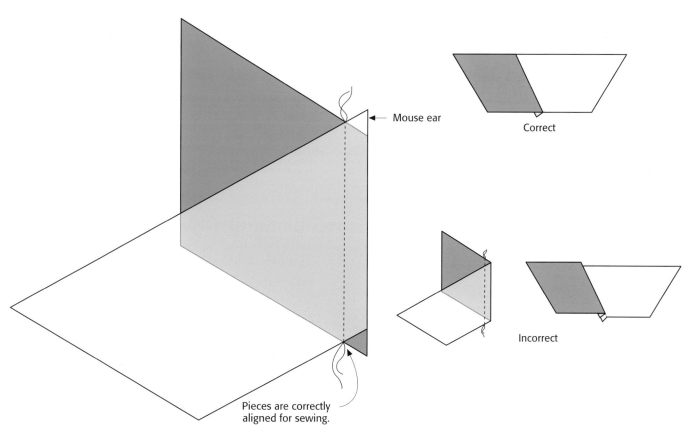

Mouse ear

Correct

Incorrect

Pieces are correctly aligned for sewing.

quilts in this book. Both square cuts and angled cuts can be made, depending on what the pattern calls for. And to take this one step further, sometimes strip-pieced units are joined and then cut at an angle for even more variety.

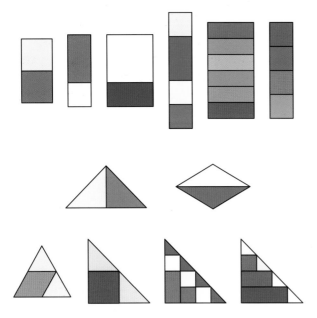

Folded Corners

The folded-corners technique has been a favorite of quilters for a number of years. This technique is typically used to add a triangle to a corner of a square, but it's a more versatile technique than that. I've even applied it to diamonds and equilateral triangles, though not in the patterns in this book.

The basic idea is to place a smaller square over the corner of a larger square with right sides together, and then sew diagonally across the smaller square. When the smaller square is folded back over itself, it creates a corner triangle. In this book, we use this basic idea to add triangles to both squares and triangles to create the units shown below.

Follow these steps to sew perfect folded corners:

1. To accurately sew across the piece you are adding, mark your machine bed with a line coming straight toward you from the needle. I'd mark the line with 5" to 6" of masking tape until I was sure it was positioned properly, and then I'd mark it with a fine-line permanent pen.

2. Place the small square of fabric over the corner of the larger piece, right sides together. When you're stitching, one corner will line up with the needle and the other corner will point right at the line. As you sew, make sure that corner exactly follows the line toward the needle.

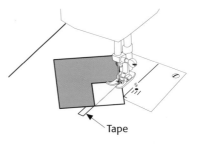

Tape

> **TIP** The folded-corners technique works well with another of my favorites: chain piecing. Just be sure that the corners of every square you feed through line up exactly on the needle and the marked line on your machine. See page 18 for details on chain piecing.

3. Gently press the square back onto itself, matching the raw edges. If it doesn't reach the corner, you need to tear out the stitches and sew a bit closer to the outside corner of the unit. If the raw edges reach past the corner, you need to sew a bit closer to the middle of the unit.

4. Trim one or both layers from behind the top triangle, leaving a ¼" seam allowance. I prefer trimming both layers to minimize bulk. Press the seam allowance toward the

smaller triangle, unless the pattern requires the seam to be pressed in the opposite direction.

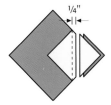 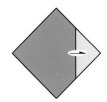

Machine Piecing

You've worked hard to make sure that your fabric patches are cut accurately, and you'll want to be just as sure that they're pieced accurately. This section will teach you the techniques you need to know for fast and accurate piecing.

The Quilter's Quarter Inch

Determining the exact width of the quilter's ¼" seam allowance is important for ensuring crisp points and perfectly matched seam intersections. It's a good idea to do this exercise before starting, to make sure you have it right.

Cut three pieces of fabric, each 1½" x 5". Use a scant ¼" seam allowance to sew them together along their long edges as shown. Press and measure the width of the three-strip unit. It should now measure exactly 3½" wide, with the center strip measuring 1" wide. If it does not, repeat the test, adjusting the seam allowance by taking a slightly wider or narrower seam until you find the correct width.

When the correct seam allowance is used, you will see that it is actually a scant ¼" wide, or a quilter's ¼". It is necessary to consistently use this seam allowance in order to obtain the correct finished dimensions of any rotary-cut project.

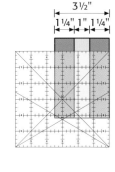

On some machines, finding and following your ¼" seam allowance is as simple as lining your fabric up with a quilting presser foot or moving the needle to the correct position. Additionally, you can mark the throat plate of

your machine with several layers of masking tape once you've found where to properly position your fabric. Feeding the fabric against the edge of the layered tape will help relieve eyestrain and help you sew more quickly. If you'd rather have a permanent line marked on your machine, repeat the test above with the tape in place to be certain it is positioned accurately before marking with a fine-line permanent pen. This is important because some machines feed the fabric at an angle and the seam width can be affected.

TIP To adjust the tape, place another piece of tape alongside the first piece on the side opposite the direction you need to move it. This way you can see how much you have actually moved it, and you won't put it right back where you had it.

Matching Seams

Every quilter aspires to perfect points. Aligning the pieces properly for sewing is a big step toward achieving perfect points. Wherever possible, align both raw edges at a corner of the patches to be sewn together as shown. The seam usually intersects where the edges of the pieces meet. Backstitching at the ends of seams is not necessary if they will be crossed by another seam. (For proper alignment of 60° patchwork, see the illustration on page 15.)

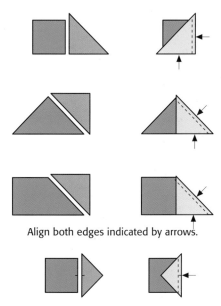

Align both edges indicated by arrows.

Align the center of each edge.

I like to see where the needle is going every stitch of the way. For the best control, use an open-toe presser foot, which is available for some machines. For my machine, I had my husband use a file from his workshop to widen the space between the toes of my presser foot to $3/32$".

Chain Piecing

When sewing a number of units that are all the same, it will save time and thread if you chain piece. Basically, this means sewing one seam right after the other rather than stopping to clip threads after each seam. With a little organization, even quilts in which each block uses different fabrics can be chain pieced.

To chain piece, spread out the block pieces following the quilt diagram. Stack identical pieces together. Pick up two pieces to be sewn together and place them with their right sides together, making sure they are correctly positioned. Set them aside and line up the next two pieces. Place them on top of the first pair, offsetting them slightly so that later, after all the pieces are paired, each pair will be easy to pick up. Stack each pair in approximately the same position so that when sewing, you always feed the same edge with the same piece on top into the machine.

When you have paired up all the pieces, begin sewing them together, checking to be sure you are sewing along the correct edge. Resist the temptation to open every pair before sewing the next pair. As long as the previous seam was sewn along the correct edge, use it as a guide for feeding the next pair. Don't lift the presser foot between pairs of patches, just continue to sew one pair after another.

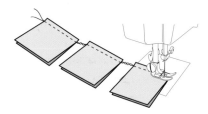

The pieces will be chained together with twisted threads between the pairs. This is preferable to lots of thread ends to trim. Snip the pieces apart and press. Continue to stack your sewn pairs in one position to help keep things organized. Soon you will be sewing the pairs into blocks and rows and adding borders.

Pressing

When pressing, remember that the heat of the iron should set the seams in the direction you want them to go; do not use force to push the iron around and stretch the edges. Instead, gently glide the iron in the direction the threads run to help prevent stretched bias edges. Generally, press the seam allowances toward the darker fabrics. Pressing the seam allowances in the direction of least resistance is the next general rule. If twisted seams result, there is no reason to worry. This is OK, and you'll get over it. Simply apply a little steam as you iron to flatten the seam all the more. Throughout the projects I've given some pressing suggestions, indicated by arrows in the illustrations. These directions will result in seams that will oppose one another and will make matching the seams practically effortless. In a few instances, I recommend pressing the seams open to minimize bulk. This is particularly helpful for small pieces or if the project will be machine quilted. Finally, a few blocks have a seam that needs to be cut in the center so that half the seam can be pressed toward one side and half the seam can be pressed toward the other. Instructions for clipping and pressing these seams are given in the individual projects.

Setting Blocks Together

The blocks are finished and it's time to set them together. Take a few minutes to play with them, if you like, and try different settings. A design wall is handy for this and helps to keep the blocks in order. Following the quilt plan, rearrange the blocks until you're happy with the color placement.

Straight-Set Quilt Assembly

The following directions will speed the process of sewing the blocks together and work well for any straight-set quilt.

1. Mentally label the blocks in columns and rows as shown.

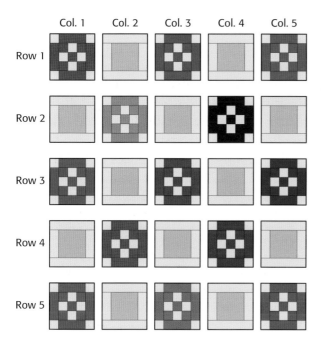

2. Stack the blocks in each column (right sides up and top edge up), working from row 1 at the top of the quilt to the bottom row. You should have as many stacks as you do columns. Use a pin to indicate the top edge of the blocks and to hold each stack together.

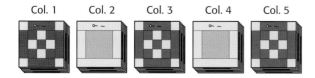

3. Take the stacked columns 1 and 2 to the sewing machine. Be careful to keep the stacks in the proper positions, with the tops of the blocks up. With right sides together, sew the first block in column 1 to the first block in column 2. Continue to chain stitch the blocks in column 1 to the blocks in column 2, sewing the blocks into rows of two blocks each. Leave the blocks chained together.

4. Bring column 3 to the machine. Keeping the stack in position, with the top of the blocks up, add the first block in the pile to row 1, the second block to row 2, and so on. You will now have rows with three blocks across, as shown, and two columns left to add. Sew all the stacks into rows. Do not clip stitches between rows.

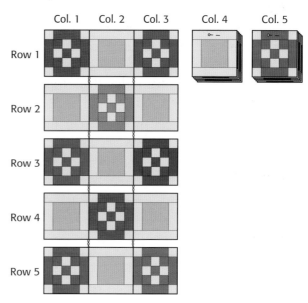

5. If all the blocks are the same, press all the seams in one row in the same direction, then press all the seams in the next row in the opposite direction. Continue pressing in alternating directions from row to row. If it's a two-block quilt, always press the seams toward the same block, such as always toward the darker block. Sew the rows together, butting the seams.

Diagonal Quilt Assembly

Quilts set on point are assembled one diagonal row at a time. The rows start short, get progressively longer, and then get shorter again. The rows begin and end with triangles called setting triangles.

There are several variations on diagonally set quilts; this book has two. "Snow Day" on page 36 has sashing and cornerstones, and "Crossed Tracks" on page 66 is a bar quilt. Construction for each quilt is the same—a skinny row and a wide row need to be sewn together before the setting triangles are added for that row. However, "Snow Day" uses just side setting triangles (large quarter-square triangles) and "Crossed Tracks" uses both side setting triangles and corner triangles (large half-square triangles).

Side setting triangles

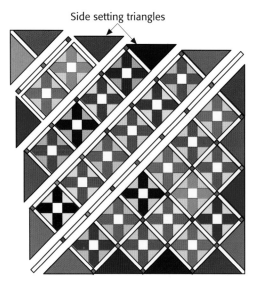

Snow Day

Side setting triangles

Corner triangle

Crossed Tracks

When sewing the triangles to the ends of each row, place the triangles underneath the row, against your machine's feed dogs. The long bias edges of triangles tend to stretch during sewing, but the feed dogs will prevent this. Add the four corner triangles last.

After the rows are sewn together, trim the outside edges of the quilt before adding any borders. As you trim the edges, keep the corners of the blocks a consistent distance from the edge on all four sides.

Borders

When making scrap quilts, I usually recommend waiting until the piecework is done before choosing a border fabric. That way you can choose a border fabric that complements the body of the quilt, rather than calls attention to itself. Each project's directions will tell you which method was used to attach the borders to the quilt shown. However, the fabric requirements listed in the patterns allow for either mitered or straight-cut borders, so feel free to choose your favorite look.

Border strips are generally cut crosswise, selvage to selvage, and joined end to end where necessary for the required length. Backstitch these short seams and press the seam allowances open so they lie flat and are less conspicuous. Try to place the seams randomly around the quilt border to make them even less noticeable.

Sewing border strips to the quilt top without measuring properly can easily make your borders as much as 3" too long. If borders on opposite sides of your quilt are different lengths, the quilt won't have square corners and won't lie flat. This extra fullness is not easily quilted out and results in wavy or rippling borders.

Straight-Cut Borders

Follow these instructions to add straight-cut borders to your quilt.

1. Measure through the center of the quilt and along the two parallel edges to find the average length. I measure using the actual border strip rather than a ruler. I mark the

three lengths with pins and compare them. Then I cut two border strips to the average length.

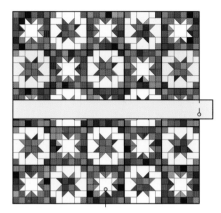

Mark the width with a pin.

2. Fold the two border strips in half and mark their centers with pins.

3. Fold your quilt in half in both directions and mark the center of each edge with a pin.

4. Matching the centers, sew the borders to opposite sides of your quilt.

5. Repeat the process for the two remaining borders, measuring through the borders you just added.

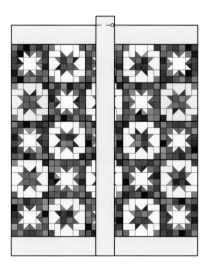

Mark the length with a pin.

Mitered Borders

Follow these instructions to add mitered borders to your quilt.

1. Calculate the length of *each* border by measuring the edge of the quilt top and adding two times the width of the borders plus 4". Sew the border strips together end to end as needed to equal the length needed for each edge.

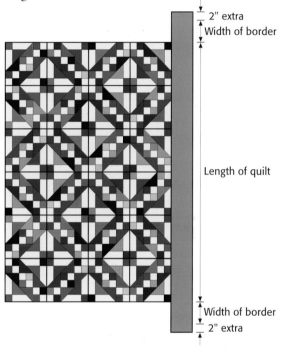

2" extra
Width of border

Length of quilt

Width of border
2" extra

2. Fold the quilt in half to find the center of each edge and mark each center with a safety pin. Fold each border strip in half to find and mark its center with a safety pin.

3. Measure the length and width of the quilt top across the center and note the measurements. Mark the border strips with a pin at each end to indicate the length of the quilt top, measuring from the center out. (Measure half the length in each direction.)

4. With right sides together, pin one border in place, matching the centers and ends of the quilt and border. Ease to fit if necessary. Sew the border to the quilt top, starting and backstitching ¼" from the first corner and stopping and backstitching ¼" from the opposite corner as shown. (For successful

mitered corners, make sure the stitching comes up to but does not extend into the ¼" seam allowance.) An open-toe foot on your sewing machine makes this step easier. Press the seam allowances toward the border. Repeat for each side.

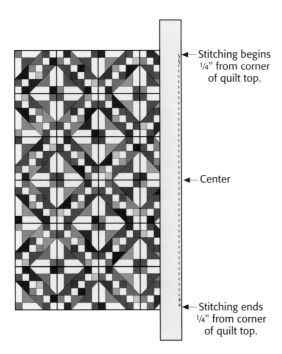

Stitching begins ¼" from corner of quilt top.

Center

Stitching ends ¼" from corner of quilt top.

5. With the quilt top right side up, pin one edge of the quilt top to your ironing board cover to help support the fabric's weight. Fold the end of the border that lies lengthwise on the ironing board at a 45° angle to the adjacent border, matching the long raw edges and placing right sides together. Use a ruler to make sure the corner is square. Press the fold. Pin the fabric together along the fold and remove the quilt top from the ironing board.

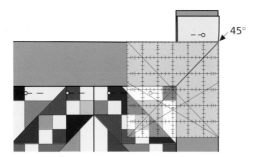

45°

Align the fold under the ruler's 45° angle.

6. With right sides together, carefully repin the fold on the back of the quilt top. Use a ruler and pencil to draw a line on the fold. Stitch the seam on that line, backstitching at the beginning and end of the seam. Do not stitch into the seam allowance. Trim the excess border fabric, leaving a ¼" seam allowance. Press this seam open. Repeat for each corner.

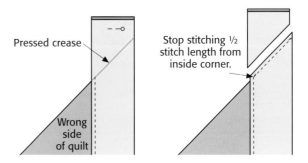

Pressed crease

Wrong side of quilt

Stop stitching ½ stitch length from inside corner.

Finishing the Quilt

The quilt top is done—now it's time to make it a real quilt! Suggested quilting designs are included with each project in this book. Feel free to change the design to suit your taste.

Marking for Quilting

Quilting motifs can be marked before or after basting, depending on the marking method used. Be sure that whatever method you use can be removed. Hand quilters generally need only a faint line from a marking pencil, chalk, or a Hera marker. Machine quilters usually use a bolder line because it is easier to see. Quilting stencils are convenient, but when one isn't available for the design I've chosen, I make my own using template plastic. You could also trace the quilting design onto a tear-away product that is removed after machine quilting. Choose the method that is right for you based on the pattern and technique you're using.

Quilt Backs

The patterns in this book indicate the yardage required for quilt backs based on 42"-wide fabric. All backs are made about 4" larger than the finished quilt top. For large quilts, it is usually necessary to sew two or three lengths of fabric together to make a backing the required size. Remove the selvages and press the backing seams open to make quilting easier. It may be more economical to use double-wide backing fabric. You will need to determine your own yardage requirements if you choose this route.

Keep in mind that if you have your quilt professionally quilted on a long-arm machine, the backing may need to be larger than directed in this book. Consult with the quilter to determine the correct size of the backing needed and leave layering to the professional quilter.

Basting

You will need a large, flat surface for basting your quilt. If your dining room table isn't big enough, see if you can use two tables pushed together at your local quilt shop or church.

To begin, secure the backing wrong side up on a flat surface using masking tape. Spread and smooth the batting over the backing. Then center the quilt top over the batting, making sure that all the layers stay smooth and even. Make long basting stitches in horizontal and vertical rows 4" apart if you will be hand quilting. Pin baste every 4" if you will be machine quilting. Avoid basting in the marked quilting lines if you can.

Quilting

Quilting is the stitching that holds the three layers of a quilt together, and it can enhance a quilt's beauty. Whether you choose to work by hand or by machine, consider adding graceful curving quilting lines to complement the geometric patchwork designs in this book.

Hand quilting can be done in your lap, in a quilting hoop, or on a quilting frame. To hand quilt, you need quilting needles, quilting thread, a thimble, and scissors or thread snips. Begin by knotting the thread about ½" from the end. Insert the needle through the top layer of the quilt only, ½" in front of where you wish to begin stitching. Tug at the thread to pop the knot into the batting.

Use the thimble to push the needle through all three layers, taking tiny, even stitches. Do not hold the needle with your finger and thumb while taking stitches. Instead, use the thumb of the hand on top of the quilt to help control the stitch length by placing it in front of the needle. Use the hand underneath the quilt to help push the needle back to the front. With practice, you should be able to get three or four stitches on the needle each time you push it through.

End a line of stitching by making a knot close to the fabric and inserting the needle back into the same hole where the last stitch came out. Travel between the layers a needle's length and come out on top. Gently pop the knot between the layers. Clip the threads close to the top. If the quilting ends near a seam, insert the needle again and travel one more inch before clipping the thread.

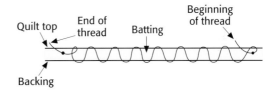

Machine quilting is a quicker way to secure the layers. I like to machine quilt using cotton thread that matches the quilt top. Most machine quilting is done using a darning foot with the machine's feed dogs dropped or covered.

Many excellent books are available to help you perfect your quilting skills, but if at all possible, I suggest you take a class. Not only are they inspiring and fun, but you can learn a lot from the hands-on experience.

Binding

After completing the quilting, machine baste in the seam allowance along all four edges of the quilt. Trim the batting and backing even with the top, and bind the quilt.

1. Referring to the cutting chart for the quilt you're making, cut the number of 2¼" strips required to bind the quilt. Cut each end of each strip at the same 45° angle.

Join all the strips end to end and press the seams open. Fold and press the strip in half lengthwise, wrong sides together. Open up and press under ¼" at the beginning of the binding. Refold the beginning end of the strip.

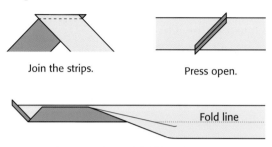

Join the strips.

Press open.

Fold line

Press under ¼" at the end, fold lengthwise, and press.

2. Place the binding strip on top of your layered quilt, aligning the raw edges. Place the beginning of the strip about 20" from the corner of the quilt. Using a ¼" seam allowance, start stitching about 3" from the beginning of the binding. Sew through both layers of binding and all three layers of the quilt. Keep the edges of the binding even with the edge of the quilt top. Stop stitching ¼" from the corner of the quilt; backstitch. Remove the quilt from under the presser foot.

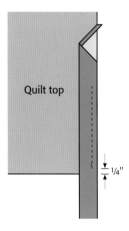

Quilt top

¼"

3. Turn the quilt so you can attach the binding to the adjacent edge of the quilt. Fold the binding strip up to be even with the right edge of the quilt, and then fold the strip down to form a pleat, placing the fold even with the top edge of the quilt. Keep the raw edges of the binding and the quilt top even.

Begin stitching again on the other side of the pleat, ¼" from the edge, and continue to ¼" from the next corner. Repeat these steps until all corners are sewn.

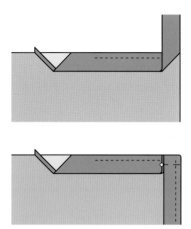

4. When you are a few inches from where you began attaching the binding, carefully cut the loose end at the correct 45° angle and tuck the end inside the beginning. Finish sewing the binding.

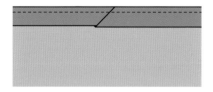

5. Turn the folded edge of the binding to the back of the quilt so it covers the row of machine stitching. Stitch the binding firmly in place with thread that matches the binding. If I quilted by hand, I sew the binding down by hand; if I quilted by machine, I sew the binding down by machine. To bind by machine, place the quilt right side up and use an open-toe presser foot with clear thread on top. Stitch in the ditch directly over the seam line, catching the fold of the binding on the back. As you approach each corner, fold the binding to form a miter and hand stitch the miter closed.

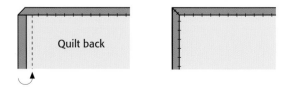

Quilt back

Signing Your Quilt

At the very least, be sure to sign and date your completed quilt with a permanent fabric-marking pen. If you want to do something more elaborate, you could make and attach a quilt label, including information such as the name of the quilt, your name, the date the quilt was completed, and who the quilt was made for. Consider making your label from a light scrap of fabric that you've also used in the quilt top. That's one more scrap out of your stash!

Making and Using a Design Wall

One of my favorite quiltmaking tools is a design wall. It gives you a great advantage when you're evaluating a design in progress because the best view of a project is straight on, not at an angle, such as when you look at it on a table, floor, or bed. Another big plus of working with a design wall is that you can stand up to work rather than getting down on your hands and knees. A design wall keeps the work visible, so it's great for monitoring your progress and inspiring yourself to continue working, and it also keeps your project out of the way of family members. It's also a great place to take photographs of your work. And a quilt top spread out on your design wall is easy to measure for borders.

A design wall is easy to use. Simply press your fabric pieces or blocks against it. The fuzzy surface grips the fabric so that pinning is not necessary. Rearranging the pieces is a snap because they don't slide out of place and you don't need to repin them as you reposition them. Remember this rule when taking blocks off the wall: Only remove what you will remember how to replace.

TIP Take a Polaroid or digital photograph to document which blocks go where in your quilt top. It's faster and easier than labeling everything.

A permanent design wall is ideal; if you do a lot of quilting, you'll wonder how you ever got along without one. My flannel-covered design wall is made of insulation board purchased from a home-improvement store. I have two 4' x 8' sheets of Styrofoam, each screwed to studs with two screws. I used a spray adhesive to attach flannel to the foam board and tucked the excess in around the edges. If you don't have flannel, felt is a good choice, too, and it can be tacked or stapled directly to the wall.

With the flannel or felt securely attached, a full-size, quilted quilt can hang from a design wall without a single pin. Occasionally I do use pins, though, such as when I am auditioning yardage for borders and have several layers of fabric. Pins are easy to insert and remove from a Styrofoam-core design wall.

If you don't have room for a permanent design wall, use a wall where you can remove a picture or two and temporarily hang some white flannel. Just place a few hooks in the ceiling and sew corresponding buttonholes along the top edge of the flannel. Or do as one friend of mine did and attach Velcro fastener to the edge of the flannel and tack the corresponding edge of the tape to the top of your closet door frame. Another friend framed 4' x 6' sheets of Celotex soundproofing board (also available at a home-improvement store) with wood and added hinges before covering it with flannel. Now she has a freestanding design wall that can be moved around the room or folded and stored behind a dresser. It's a good solution if you don't have the wall space to dedicate to a design wall.

bosom buddies

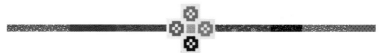

By Gayle Bong—quilted by Sue Schmeiden, the Quilting Connection

THIS WINNING COMBINATION of two simple blocks practically guarantees quilting satisfaction. The scrappy border perfectly complements the blocks and gives the quilt a comfortable, casual look, and the whole thing's a breeze to cut and piece. This is the quilt to make if you have great flannels or novelty prints you want to showcase.

Block A

Block B

Finished quilt: 66½" x 86½"
Finished blocks: 10"

Materials

Yardages are based on 42"-wide fabric.

- 2⅝ yards *total* of assorted dark scraps for block A and border
- 2½ yards of cream for block backgrounds
- 1⅜ yards of medium gold for block B and inner border
- 5½ yards for backing
- ¾ yard for binding
- 72" x 92" piece of batting

Cutting

Please read all the directions before starting.

FABRIC	FIRST CUT	ADDITIONAL CUTS
Assorted Dark Scraps	18 strips, 2½" x 42"	4 rectangles, 2½" x 6½", and 5 squares, 2½" x 2½", from *each* strip
	4½" strips of various lengths*	
Cream	9 strips, 2½" x 42"	144 squares, 2½" x 2½"
	6 strips, 2½" x 42"	
	2 strips, 10½" x 42"	32 rectangles, 2½" x 10½"
	1 strip, 14½" x 42"	16 rectangles, 2½" x 14½"**
Medium Gold	3 strips, 6½" x 42"	
	2 strips, 2½" x 42"	10 rectangles, 2½" x 6½"
	7 strips, 2½" x 42"	
Binding	8 strips, 2¼" x 42"	

Additional Cutting

*Cut the 4½"-wide scraps into various lengths for the border. You will need the equivalent of 18 pieces 18" long.
**Trim four of the rectangles to 2½" x 12½" and trim another two rectangles to 2½" x 10½". Set the 2½" x 10½" rectangles with the other 32 rectangles of the same size.

Making Block A

1. Make a nine-patch unit using five identical dark 2½" squares and four cream 2½" squares. Sew the squares into rows and sew the rows together. Repeat to make 18 nine-patch units.

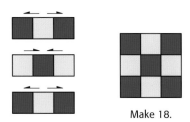

Make 18.

2. Add two matching dark 2½" x 6½" rectangles to opposite sides of each nine patch.

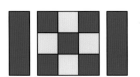

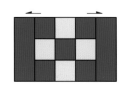

3. Sew two cream 2½" squares to opposite sides of the remaining two matching dark rectangles. Sew the units to opposite sides of the unit made in step 2. Make 18.

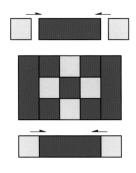

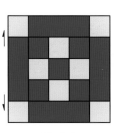

Block A.
Make 18.

Making Block B

1. Sew a 2½" x 42" cream strip to each side of a 6½" medium gold strip. Repeat to make three strip sets. Cut 17 segments, 6½" each.

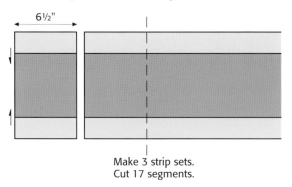

Make 3 strip sets.
Cut 17 segments.

2. Sew two 2½" x 10½" cream rectangles to opposite sides of each segment from step 1. Make 17.

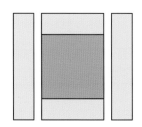

Block B.
Make 17.

Quilt Assembly and Borders

1. Arrange the blocks in rows, alternating them as shown in the quilt assembly diagram on page 29. Play with their arrangement until you're happy with the color placement. Sew the blocks into rows; then sew the rows together.

2. Sew four border strips together, alternating the 2½" x 6½" gold rectangles with the 2½" x 12½" and 2½" x 14½" cream rectangles as shown. Sew the side borders to the quilt top; then add the top and bottom borders.

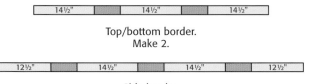

Top/bottom border.
Make 2.

Side border.
Make 2.

3. Use the 2½" gold strips to add the inner border to the quilt top, following the directions in "Straight-Cut Borders" on page 20.

4. Sew the 4½" dark strips of various lengths together end to end as needed to make each pieced border.

Piece top, bottom, and side borders to fit.

5. Follow the directions in "Straight-Cut Borders" to measure and add the pieced outer border to the quilt top. Press the seam allowances toward the gold borders.

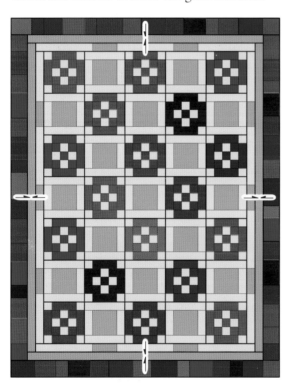

Quilt assembly

6. Sew a line of stay stitching 3/16" from the edge of the quilt to prevent the seams in the pieced border from coming loose around the edge of the quilt.

Finishing Up

1. Mark quilting lines, if desired.

2. Layer the quilt top with the batting and backing. Baste.

3. Hand or machine quilt. Follow the quilting suggestions below or use your own design.

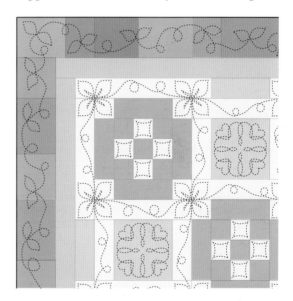

4. Refer to "Binding" on page 23 to bind the quilt.

5. Sign and date your quilt.

good neighbors

By Gayle Bong

T HREE DIFFERENT STRIP SETS let you quickly strip piece this quilt, which features just two different blocks. By making a block *and* its mirror image, you easily create this quilt's unusual zigzag pattern. I chose to use a very tight range of colors, but you could use a more varied range—such as purples, blues, and greens—and still get dramatic results, as long as you use dark prints in place of the browns and medium prints in place of the blues.

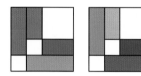

Finished quilt: 78½" x 84½"
Finished blocks: 6"

Materials

Yardages are based on 42"-wide fabric.

* 3 yards *total* of assorted brown scraps for blocks and border
* 3 yards *total* of assorted blue scraps for blocks and border
* 2¼ yards of ecru for block backgrounds
* 5 yards for backing
* ¾ yard for binding
* 84" x 90" piece of batting

Cutting

Please read all the directions before starting. Cut an assortment of prints for each step.

FABRIC	FIRST CUT	FOLLOWING CUTS
Ecru	11 strips, 3½" x 42"	
	14 strips, 2" x 42"	
	2 strips, 2" x 42"	24 squares, 2" x 2"
		2 rectangles, 2" x 3½"
Assorted Blues	17 strips, 2" x 42"	66 rectangles, 2" x 3½"; set aside the 11 remaining strips
	12 strips, 5" x 42"	228 rectangles, 2" x 5"
		4 rectangles, 2" x 3½"
Assorted Browns	7 strips, 3½" x 42"	
	7 strips, 5" x 42"	
	18 strips, 2" x 42"	77 rectangles, 2" x 3½"
		92 rectangles, 2" x 5"
		4 squares, 2" x 2"
Binding	9 strips, 2¼" x 42"	

Making the Blocks

1. Sew a 3½" ecru strip to a 2" blue strip. Repeat to make 11 sets. Cut 120 segments, 3½" each.

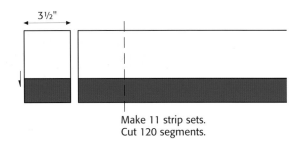

Make 11 strip sets.
Cut 120 segments.

2. Sew a 3½" brown strip to a 2" ecru strip. Repeat to make 7 sets. Cut 124 segments, 2" each. Set aside 4 segments of various prints for the center row.

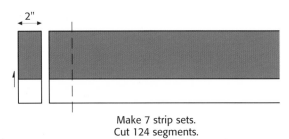

Make 7 strip sets.
Cut 124 segments.

3. Sew 60 brown segments to the left edges of 60 blue segments, and 60 brown segments to the right edges of 60 blue segments.

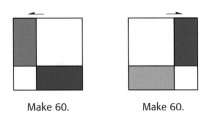

Make 60.   Make 60.

4. Sew the 2" x 5" blue rectangles to the blue edges of all 120 blocks. Set aside the remaining 108 blue 2" x 5" rectangles for the center row and border.

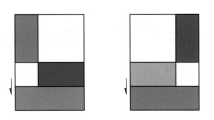

5. Sew a 5" brown strip to a 2" ecru strip. Repeat to make 7 sets. Cut 136 segments, 2" each. Set aside 16 segments of various prints for making the center row.

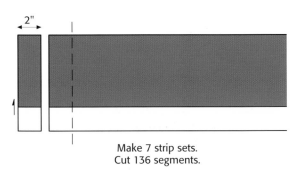

Make 7 strip sets.
Cut 136 segments.

6. Sew the 120 segments from step 5 to the brown edges of the blocks from step 4.

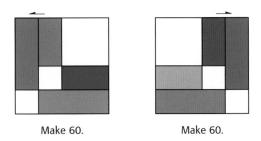

Make 60.   Make 60.

Making the Center Row

1. Sew groups of four brown segments (from step 5 of "Making the Blocks") together as shown. Repeat to make four units.

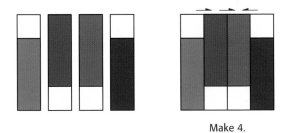

Make 4.

2. Sew the four brown squares into a four-patch and add the two 2" x 3½" ecru rectangles to opposite sides. This unit is the very center of the quilt.

 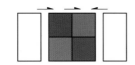

Make 1.

3. Sew two brown segments (from step 2 of "Making the Blocks") together as shown. Add a 2" x 5" brown rectangle to each side. Repeat to make two units. These units are the ends of the center vertical row.

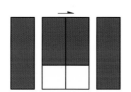 

Make 2.

4. Sew a 2" ecru square to a 2" x 5" blue rectangle as shown. Using various prints, repeat to make 24 units. Join four units together to make a blue unit; repeat to make six total.

 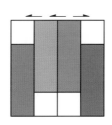

Make 6.

5. Sew the blocks together as shown below to make the center row (section A). (Note that this unit, shown horizontally here, is actually the vertical center of the quilt.)

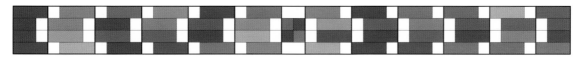

Section A

Assembling the Quilt

1. Alternating blocks, lay out and sew together six *each* of the two rows shown. Alternate rows to make two B sections.

Row 1.
Make 6.

Row 2.
Make 6.

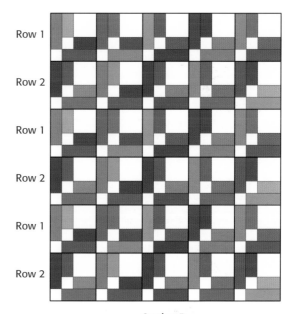

Row 1

Row 2

Row 1

Row 2

Row 1

Row 2

Section B.
Make 2.

2. Alternating blocks, lay out and sew together six *each* of the two rows shown. Alternate rows to make two C sections.

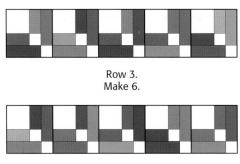

Row 3.
Make 6.

Row 4.
Make 6.

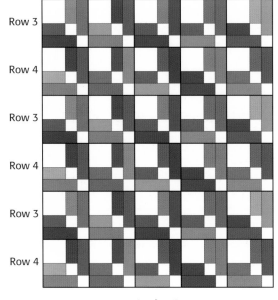

Row 3

Row 4

Row 3

Row 4

Row 3

Row 4

Section C.
Make 2.

3. Join the five sections, rotating one B section and one C section as shown to create the pattern in the photograph.

Section A

Section B

Section C

Section C

Section B

Making the Borders

1. Sew the 2" x 5" and the 2" x 3½" blue rectangles end to end, randomly alternating lengths and prints, to make a long border strip. Cut the strip in half to make two strips, and sew the two strips together to make a double-wide blue pieced border.

TIP Do not press the seams in the pieced border until after you sew the two strips together. This way you can flip the seams in whatever direction is needed so the seams butt where they meet.

2. Trim the border strips to the required lengths *as* you add them to the quilt. Line up the seams in the quilt blocks with the seams in the borders, sew them together, and then trim both ends of the border. Press the seam allowances toward the border.

3. Sew all the 2" x 5" and 2" x 3½" brown rectangles end to end, randomly alternating lengths and prints, to make a long border strip. Cut the strip in half to make two strips, and sew the two strips together to make a double-wide brown pieced border. Repeat step 2 to add the pieced outer border to the quilt.

Quilt assembly

4. Sew a line of stay stitching ³⁄₁₆" from the edge of the quilt to prevent the seams in the pieced border from coming loose around the edge of the quilt.

Finishing Up

1. Mark quilting lines, if desired.

2. Layer the quilt top with the batting and backing. Baste.

3. Hand or machine quilt. Follow the quilting suggestions below or use your own design.

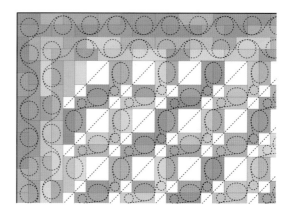

4. Refer to "Binding" on page 23 to bind the quilt.

5. Sign and date your quilt.

snow day

By Gayle Bong

T HIS BLOCK is more fun to make than the common Nine Patch, and it's just as easy. I've seen antique quilts made from this block, and I thought it would be perfect for my growing collection of 1800s reproduction prints. If you would rather be dramatic, use bold, contemporary colors and prints. I updated the traditional design with narrow sashing and scrappy setting triangles.

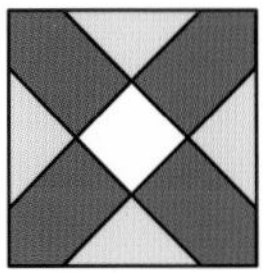

Finished quilt: 62¾" x 62¾"
Finished blocks: 9½"

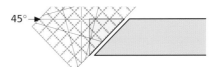

Materials

Yardages are based on 42"-wide fabric.

- 1¾ yards *total* of assorted dark scraps for blocks
- 1⅜ yards of muslin for blocks and sashing
- 1⅜ yards *total* of assorted medium scraps for blocks
- ¼ yard *each* of 8 different dark prints for blocks, setting triangles, and cornerstones
- 3¾ yards for backing
- ⅝ yard for binding
- 68" x 68" piece of batting

Cut 4 from each medium strip
and 2 from each dark strip.

Cutting

Please read all the directions before starting.

FABRIC	FIRST CUT	FOLLOWING CUTS
Dark Scraps	16 strips, 3½" x 25"	4 rectangles, 3½" x 6", from *each* strip (64 total)
Muslin	3 strips, 3½" x 42"	24 squares, 3½" x 3½"
	17 strips, 1¾" x 42"	4 rectangles, 1¾" x 12"
		60 rectangles, 1¾" x 10", for sashing
Medium Scraps	24 strips, 3½" x 18"	4 triangles from *each* strip (96 total)*
8 Different Dark Prints	8 strips, 8¼" x 42"	2 triangles from *each* strip (16 total)*
		4 rectangles, 3½" x 6", from *each* strip (32 total)
		37 squares, 1¾" x 1¾"
Binding	7 strips, 2¼" x 42"	

Additional Cutting

*Place the 45° line of your ruler on the long edge of the strip and make the first cut near the lower-left corner of the strip. Take the piece you've cut and put it in your scrap stash. Rotate the ruler so it is perpendicular to the first cut, place the 45° line on the bottom edge of the strip, and align the cutting edge of the ruler with the top edge of the strip to form a triangle. Cut. Repeat the process, alternating the ruler between these positions to cut the required triangles. (See above.)

Making the Blocks

1. For each block, sew a 3½" muslin square, four matching medium triangles, and four matching 3½" x 6" dark rectangles together as shown. Press the seam allowances away from the center square. Make 24 blocks.

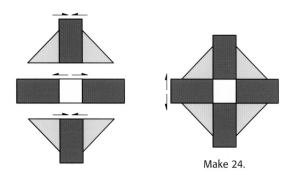

Make 24.

TIP Before you start sewing, take some time to decide which medium print triangles and dark print rectangles go best together. (Now's the time to use that design wall!) If you have all of your fabrics paired up before you begin sewing, it's easy to chain piece the diagonal rows of the blocks quickly and efficiently.

2. Square the blocks to 10", measuring 5" from the center point to trim each edge. If possible, use a large square ruler so you can measure and cut two edges without moving the ruler.

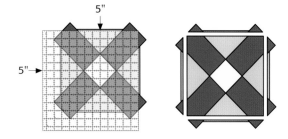

Assembling the Quilt

1. Sew a short edge of two different dark triangles to the sides of one 1¾" x 12" muslin strip as shown. The sashing strip will be longer than the triangles. Press the

seam allowances toward the triangles. Trim the excess sashing at the corner, using the edges of the triangles as a guide. Repeat to make a second corner unit.

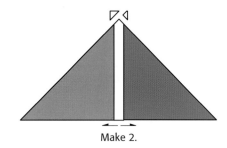

Make 2.

2. Join the blocks and 1¾" x 10" muslin strips into rows as shown in the diagram below.

3. Join the dark 1¾" squares and the 1¾" x 10" muslin strips into sashing rows as shown in the diagram below. Use the remaining two 1¾" x 12" muslin strips at the ends of the center row.

4. Sew the rows of blocks and rows of sashing strips together as shown in the diagram below. Sew the side setting triangles to the ends of the rows.

5. Square up the corners of the 1¾" x 12" muslin strips as in step 1.

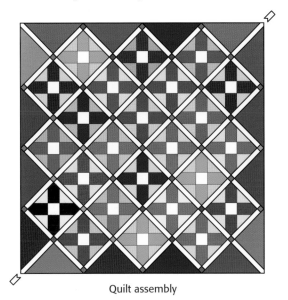

Quilt assembly

6. Sew a line of stay stitching ³⁄₁₆" from the edge of the quilt. This will prevent the seams from coming loose around the edges of the quilt.

Finishing Up

1. Mark quilting lines, if desired.

2. Layer the quilt top with the batting and backing. Baste.

3. Hand or machine quilt. Follow the quilting suggestions below or use your own design.

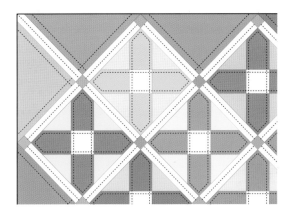

4. Refer to "Binding" on page 23 to bind the quilt.

5. Sign and date your quilt.

plan b

By Gayle Bong

To MAKE THIS QUILT I used scraps in a rainbow of colors, but this design would be just as effective if it were made in a limited color palette. Folded corners and strip piecing with staggered strip sets make this quilt fast and fun to make, and the end result is truly eye-catching.

Light-Star block   Dark-Star block

Finished quilt: 54" x 54"
Finished blocks: 9"

Materials

Yardages are based on 42"-wide fabric.

- 2 yards *total* of assorted medium and dark scraps for stars and backgrounds
- 1⅜ yards *total* of assorted light scraps for backgrounds (the equivalent of 12 strips, each 3½" x 31")
- ¾ yard *total* of light scraps for stars (the equivalent of 13 strips, each 3½" x 14")
- 1⅝ yards of dark blue for border and binding
- 3½ yards for backing
- 60" x 60" piece of batting

Cutting

Please read all the directions before starting. The light pieces don't have to be cut from strips. If you have an assortment of odd-sized scraps, just follow the last column, cutting a set of matching light pieces for each block.

FABRIC	FIRST CUT	FOLLOWING CUTS
Light Scraps for Backgrounds	12 strips, 3½" x 31"	4 squares, 3½" x 3½", from *each* strip (48 total)
		4 rectangles, 2" x 3½", from *each* strip (48 total)
		4 squares, 2" x 2", from *each* strip (48 total)
Light Scraps for Stars	13 strips, 3½" x 14"	1 square, 3½" x 3½", from *each* strip (13 total)
		4 squares, 2⅜" x 2⅜", from *each* strip (52 total). Cut each square in half once diagonally to yield 104 triangles.
Medium and Dark Scraps	52 squares, 2⅜" x 2⅜"	Cut each square in half once diagonally to yield 104 triangles
	196 squares, 2" x 2"	
	36 strips, 2" x 20"	
Dark Blue	6 strips, 5" x 42"	
	6 strips, 2¼" x 42"	

Making the Light-Star Blocks

1. Join a 2⅜" light triangle and a 2⅜" dark triangle to make a half-square-triangle unit. Repeat to make 104 units. Keep sets of 8 matching light half-square triangles together.

Make 104.

2. Sew a pair of half-square-triangle units together as shown. Press the seam allowance open. Repeat to make 52 pairs, keeping the matching light-triangle units together.

Make 52.

3. Sew medium or dark 2" squares to both ends of two matching units from step 2. Sew the remaining two matching units to opposite sides of a matching light 3½" square. Sew the rows together as shown to make light stars. Repeat to make 13 units.

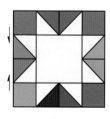

Make 13.

4. Sew the 2" x 20" medium and dark strips together into 18 pairs. Press the seams to either side. Sew three pairs of strips together, staggering the ends about 10" as shown. Press to either side. Repeat to make six staggered sets. Cut the strip sets into 2"

wide segments. You'll need 50 two-square segments and 52 four-square segments. Set aside 24 two-square segments for the centers of the dark stars.

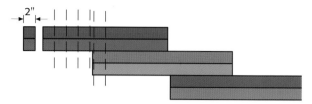

Make 6 sets of 6 strips each.

Cut 50.

Cut 52.

5. Sew two units with four squares to opposite sides of a star. Press the seams away from the star. Repeat to make 13.

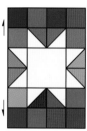

Make 13.

6. Sew a unit with two squares to one end of each remaining unit with four squares. Before pressing, sew the resulting units to the remaining two sides of a star. (If you wait to press, then the seams can be flipped to butt the seams in the center.) Make 13 Light-Star blocks.

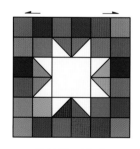

Light-Star block.
Make 13.

Making the Dark-Star Blocks

1. Sew together the two-square units you set aside in step 4 on the opposite page to make 12 four-patch units.

Make 12.

2. Sew a 2" medium or dark square to a 2" light square; then add a 2" x 3½" light rectangle. Repeat to make 48 units, keeping matching light fabrics together.

Make 48.

3. Using the folded-corners technique (see page 16 for details), sew 2" medium or dark squares to adjacent corners of a 3½" light square to make the dark-star points. Repeat to make 48 star-point units.

Make 48.

4. Sew a unit from step 2 to each side of a star-point unit from step 3, positioning the units exactly as shown, to make rows 1 and 3 of each block. Sew a star-point unit to each side of a four-patch unit from step 1,

positioning the units as shown, to make row 2. Sew the rows together. Repeat to make 12 Dark-Star blocks.

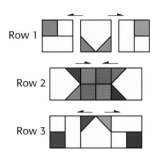 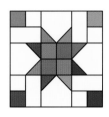

Dark-Star block.
Make 12.

Quilt Assembly and Borders

1. Arrange the blocks on your design wall, alternating Light-Star and Dark-Star blocks as shown in the quilt assembly diagram below. Play with the position of the blocks until you are happy with the color arrangement. Sew the blocks into rows, pressing the seams in adjacent rows in opposite directions. Sew the rows together.

2. Using the dark blue 5" x 42" strips, add the border to the quilt top. The quilt shown has mitered borders; refer to page 20 to attach the borders using whatever method you prefer.

Quilt assembly

Finishing Up

1. Mark quilting lines, if desired.

2. Layer the quilt top with the batting and backing. Baste.

3. Hand or machine quilt. Follow the quilting suggestions shown at right or use your own design.

4. Refer to "Binding" on page 23 to bind the quilt.

5. Sign and date your quilt.

PLANS C, D, AND E

If you'd like to make a bigger quilt, or if you have a lot of large scraps, follow one of these plans. Keep in mind that you'll need larger quantities of the border, backing, and binding fabrics, plus a larger piece of batting. Because you may want to adjust the width of the border to be proportional to whatever block size you choose, quilt sizes given here are calculated *without* the borders included.

FINISHED BLOCK SIZE	SIZE TO CUT THE PATCHES				ALTERNATE QUILT SIZES (without borders)		
	Small Squares and Strips	Large Squares	Triangles*	Light Rectangles	Number of Blocks	Block Layout	Quilt Size
9" (same as sample quilt)	2"	3½"	2⅜"	2" x 3½"	25 light stars + 24 dark stars	7 blocks x 7 blocks	63" x 63"
12"	2½"	4½"	2⅞"	2½" x 4½"	13 light stars + 12 dark stars OR 18 light stars + 17 dark stars	5 blocks x 5 blocks OR 5 blocks x 7 blocks	60" x 60" OR 60" x 84"
15"	3"	5½"	3⅜"	3" x 5½"	13 light stars + 12 dark stars	5 blocks x 5 blocks	75" x 75"

For the triangles, cut squares the size listed and then cut the squares in half once diagonally.

geese in the garden

By Gayle Bong

I CAREFULLY CHOSE THESE SCRAPS so the medium fabrics would echo the designs of the darker fabrics. The border fabric set off my scraps better than any other print could have, so I actually stole it away from a different quilt top in my collection! Making this quilt is easier than it looks because you use the folded-corners technique and then trim the units to shape after sewing. If you carefully follow the pressing plan, your blocks will go together smoothly.

Finished quilt: 49½" x 49½"
Finished blocks: 6"

Materials

Yardages are based on 42"-wide fabric.

- 1½ yards of multicolored large-scale print for outer border
- 1¼ yards *total* of assorted medium scraps for blocks
- 1¼ yards *total* of assorted dark scraps for blocks
- 1⅛ yards of muslin for background
- ⅜ yard of dark blue print for inner border
- 3 yards for backing
- ½ yard for the binding
- 55" x 55" piece of batting

TIP If you want to make more blocks for a larger quilt, you'll need ⅜ yard of 42" muslin for every three blocks.

Cutting

Please read all the directions before starting.

FABRIC	FIRST CUT	FOLLOWING CUTS
Medium Scraps	72 rectangles, 1½" x 5"	
	72 rectangles, 1½" x 7"	
Muslin	3 strips, 3" x 42"	36 squares, 3" x 3"; cut *each* square in half once diagonally to yield 72 triangles
	9 strips, 2½" x 42"	144 squares, 2½" x 2½"
Dark Scraps	72 rectangles, 1½" x 5"	
	72 rectangles, 1½" x 7"	
Dark Blue Print	4 strips, 2½" x 42"	
Multicolored Large-Scale Print	4 lengthwise-cut strips, 5" x 54"	
Binding	5 strips, 2¼" x 42"	

Making the Blocks

Each block is first assembled as two half blocks.

Half-Block A

Press all the seams in Half-Block A toward the center triangle. All squaring up will be done after the half block is sewn.

1. Sew a 1½" x 5" medium rectangle to a muslin triangle, matching the top edge as shown. Press. Repeat to make 36 units.

Make 36.

2. Sew a 1½" x 5" dark rectangle to the other short side of the muslin triangle, matching the edge at the corner of the first rectangle as shown. Repeat on all 36 units.

Make 36.

3. Referring to "Folded Corners" on page 16, sew a 2½" muslin square over the corner of the unit. Trim and press the seam allowance as shown. Repeat on all 36 units.

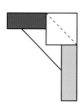 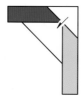

Make 36.

4. Sew a 1½" x 7" medium rectangle next to the first medium rectangle as shown, matching the edge at the corner of the muslin triangle. Repeat on all 36 units.

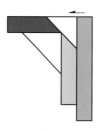

Make 36.

5. Sew a 1½" x 7" dark rectangle next to the first dark rectangle as shown, matching the short end with the long edge of the medium rectangle. Repeat on all 36 units.

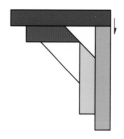

Make 36.

6. As in step 3, sew a 2½" muslin square over the corner of the unit. Trim and press the seam allowance as shown.

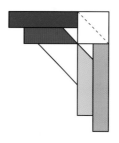 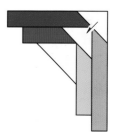

Make 36.

7. If you have a triangle rotary ruler, use it to measure and trim the bias edge of the block by measuring the short sides to 6⅞". If you don't have a triangle ruler, use a square ruler to trim each short edge to 6½". Then, using a long rotary ruler, align the corners of the unit with the ¼" line on the ruler as shown. Trim all 36 half blocks.

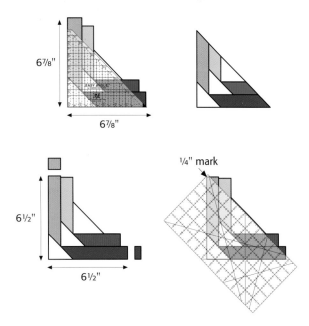

Half-Block B

Press all the seams in Half-Block B away from the center triangle. All squaring up will be done after the half block is sewn, just as with Half-Block A.

1. Sew a 1½" x 5" dark rectangle to a muslin triangle, matching the top edge as shown. Press. Repeat to make 36 units.

Make 36.

2. Sew a 1½" x 5" medium rectangle to the other short side of the muslin triangle, matching the edge at the corner of the first rectangle. Press. Repeat on all 36 units.

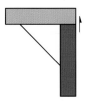

Make 36.

3. Use the folded-corners technique to sew a muslin square over the corner. Trim and press the seam allowance as shown. Repeat on all 36 units.

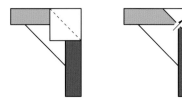

Make 36.

4. Sew a 1½" x 7" dark rectangle next to the first dark rectangle, matching the edge at the corner of the muslin triangle. Press. Repeat on all 36 units.

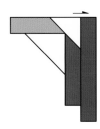

Make 36.

5. Sew a 1½" x 7" medium rectangle next to the first medium rectangle, matching the short end with the long edge of the dark rectangle. Press. Repeat on all 36 units.

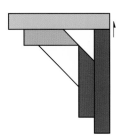

Make 36.

6. Use the folded-corners technique to sew a muslin square over the corner of the half block. Trim and press the seam allowance as shown. Repeat on all 36 units.

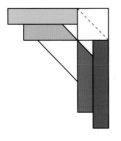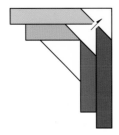

Make 36.

7. Trim every Half-Block B in the same manner as you trimmed Half-Block A in step 7 on page 48.

Make 36.

Quilt Assembly and Borders

1. Sew one Half-Block A to one Half-Block B. Press seams to either side. Repeat to make 36 blocks.

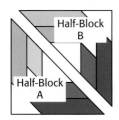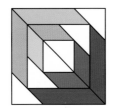

Half-Block B

Half-Block A

Make 36.

2. Arrange the blocks as shown in the quilt assembly diagram at upper right. When you are happy with the color placement, sew the blocks into rows and sew the rows together.

3. Using the dark blue print for the inner border and the multicolored large-scale print for the outer border, add the borders to the quilt top. The quilt shown on page 45 has straight-cut borders, but we've

illustrated it below with mitered borders (the author's preference). Refer to page 20 to attach your borders using whatever method you prefer.

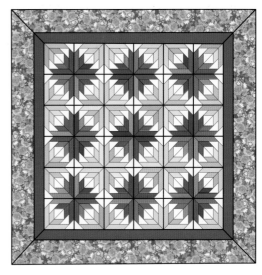

Quilt assembly

Finishing Up

1. Mark quilting lines, if desired.

2. Layer the quilt top with the batting and backing. Baste.

3. Hand or machine quilt. Follow the quilting suggestions shown below or use your own design.

4. Refer to "Binding" on page 23 to bind the quilt.

5. Sign and date your quilt.

full house

By Gayle Bong

M OST QUILTERS will find that their stashes are full of fabrics that are just perfect for this quilt. "Full House" is a great place to showcase large-scale patterns and novelty prints, which sometimes have a hard time finding homes in other scrap quilts. The flying-geese border units create a rickrack effect, drawing your eye around the quilt and giving you lots of opportunities to use up those orphaned scraps.

Finished quilt: 56½" x 72½"
Finished blocks: 16"

Materials

Yardages are based on 42"-wide fabric.

- 3¼ yards *total* of assorted medium and dark scraps

- 2½ yards of tan

- 3½ yards for backing

- ⅝ yard for binding

- 62" x 78" piece of batting

Making the Blocks

1. Using the folded-corners technique (see page 16 for details), sew two 2½" tan background squares onto opposite corners of a 4½" medium or dark square. Repeat to make 48 folded-corner units.

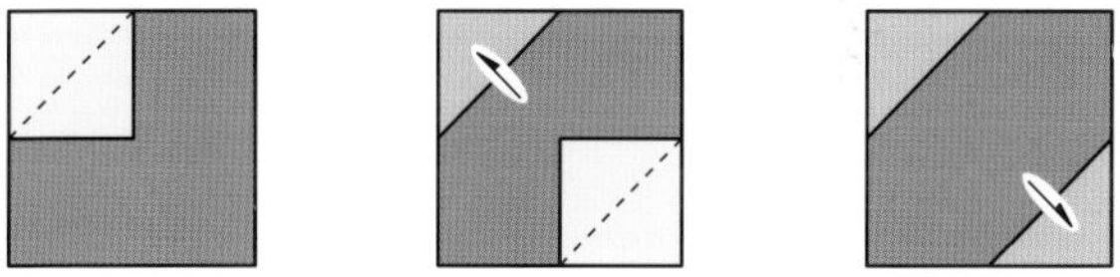

Make 48.

Cutting
Please read all the directions before starting.

FABRIC	FIRST CUT	FOLLOWING CUTS
Tan	6 strips, 2½" x 42"	96 squares, 2½" x 2½"
	7 strips, 4⅞" x 42"	52 squares, 4⅞" x 4⅞"; cut *each* square in half once diagonally to yield 104 triangles
	3 strips, 3½" x 42"	Cut strips in half to yield 6 strips, 3½" x 21"
	2 strips, 9¼" x 42"	6 squares, 9¼" x 9¼"; cut *each* square in half twice diagonally to yield 24 triangles
	4 squares, 4½" x 4½"	
Medium and Dark Scraps	48 squares, 4½" x 4½"	
	13 strips, 4⅞" x 42"	100 squares, 4⅞" x 4⅞"; cut *each* square in half once diagonally to yield 200 triangles
	6 strips, 2½" x 21"	
Binding	7 strips, 2¼" x 42"	

2. Sew a 4⅞" tan and a 4⅞" medium or dark triangle together to make a half-square-triangle unit. Repeat to make 104 units. Set aside 8 units in various prints for the border.

Make 104.

3. Sew a 2½" medium or dark strip to a 3½" tan strip. Press the seam allowances toward the dark strips. Repeat to make six strip sets. Cut 48 segments, each 2½" wide.

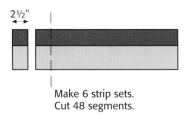

2½"

Make 6 strip sets.
Cut 48 segments.

4. Sew two of the 2½" segments from step 3 together to make an uneven four-patch unit as shown. Note that the seams will not meet in the center. Turn the piece over and snip into the seam allowance in the center of the seam. Press each half of the seam allowance toward a dark square. Repeat to make 24 uneven four patches.

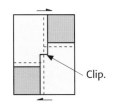

Clip.

Make 24.

5. Using a triangle rotary ruler, cut each uneven four patch into two triangle units. Measure a 4⅞" triangle as shown and cut along the diagonal edge. Rotate the remaining piece, measure, and cut another 4⅞" triangle. (There is a little bit of waste

between the units and a tip of each unit will be missing, but the seam allowance is large enough that this doesn't pose a problem.) Cut 48 triangle units.

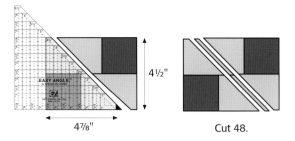

4½"

4⅞"

Cut 48.

An alternate method, if you don't have a triangle-cutting tool, is to mark your standard ruler with a cutting guide. To begin, cut out a 4⅞" square of paper. Cut the square in half once diagonally. Flip your ruler over so the wrong side is facing up and position the paper template on your ruler, lining up the long edge of the template with the cutting edge of your ruler. Hold the paper in position and place a piece of masking tape *next to* the two edges of the template; do not tape the template down. Remove the paper template. Triangles cut with this system should fit inside the taped edges. Simply butt the fabric against both tape guides and cut along the ruler's edge.

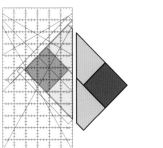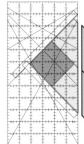

6. Sew a medium or dark 4⅞" triangle to a triangle unit from step 5. Repeat to make 48 units. Press the seam allowances toward the dark triangles.

Make 48.

7. Join all the units into 48 quarter blocks as shown; then join four quarters to complete a block. Make 12 blocks.

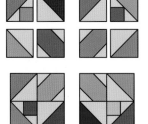 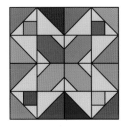

Make 12.

Quilt Assembly and Borders

1. Sew the blocks into three rows of four blocks each; then sew the rows together.

2. Sew 4⅞" medium or dark triangles to the short sides of the tan 9¼" triangles to make a flying-geese unit. Press one seam allowance toward the tan and one toward the dark fabric. Repeat to make 24 units.

Make 24.

3. Sew the flying-geese units, half-square-triangle units, and 4½" tan squares end to end as shown to make the pieced borders. Sew the longer borders to the quilt sides, and then sew the shorter borders to the top and bottom of the quilt.

Top/bottom border.
Make 2.

Side border.
Make 2.

TIP Do not press the seam allowances between the units in the pieced border until you sew the border to the quilt. Then flip the seams so they oppose the seams between the blocks.

4. Sew a line of stay stitching 3/16" from the edge of the quilt. This will prevent the seams in the pieced border from coming loose around the edge of the quilt.

Quilt assembly

Finishing Up

1. Mark quilting lines, if desired.

2. Layer the quilt top with the batting and backing. Baste.

3. Hand or machine quilt. Follow the quilting suggestions below or use your own design.

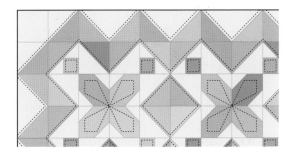

4. Refer to "Binding" on page 23 to bind the quilt.

5. Sign and date your quilt.

summer spirit

By Gayle Bong

I'VE LOOKED at so many patterns during my 20 years of quiltmaking that it's hard to know whether this is a new design or just one that was filed away in my memory. Reminiscent of a Jacob's Ladder design, this quilt features light crosses and a chain of squares marching through the scraps. If you love the pattern but your scrap stash is running low, make a smaller, lap-sized version (see page 57).

Finished quilt: 80½" x 104½"
Finished blocks: 12"

Materials

Yardages are based on 42"-wide fabric.

- 4⅝ yards total of assorted medium and dark scraps for the blocks

- 4½ yards of cream for crosses and chain of squares

- 1¾ yards of multicolored print for border

- 7½ yards for backing

- ¾ yard for binding

- 86" x 110" piece of batting

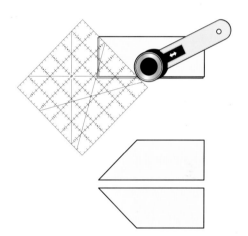

Cutting

Please read all the directions before starting.

FABRIC	FIRST CUT	FOLLOWING CUTS
Cream	18 strips, 2½" x 42"	
	14 strips, 6⅞" x 42"	With strips folded once, cut a total of 192 rectangles, each 2½" x 6⅞"*
Medium and Dark Scraps	18 strips, 2½" x 42"	
	96 squares, 2½" x 2½"	
	18 strips, 4⅞" x 42"	144 squares, 4⅞" x 4⅞"; cut *each* square in half once diagonally to yield 288 triangles
Multicolored Print	7 lengthwise-cut strips, 4½"	
Binding	10 strips, 2¼" x 42"	

With pairs of rectangles wrong sides together, trim a 45° triangle from one end, leaving a pair of mirror-image trapezoids. (See above.)

Making the Blocks

1. Sew a 2½" cream strip to a 2½" medium or dark strip. Repeat to make 18 strip sets. Press the seam allowances toward the dark fabrics. Layer two or three sets as shown, offsetting each about ½" to distribute the bulk created by the seam allowances. Cut the strip sets into 2½"-wide units. Join the units as shown, mixing colors randomly, to make 144 scrappy four-patch units.

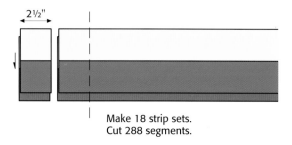

Make 18 strip sets.
Cut 288 segments.

Make 144.

2. Join two mirror-image trapezoids, a medium or dark 2½" square, and a medium or dark 4⅞" triangle as shown to make a corner unit. Repeat to make 96 corner units.

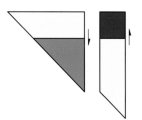

Make 96.

3. Join the four-patch units from step 1 and the medium and dark 4⅞" triangles to make 48 of each of the units shown.

Make 48.   Make 48.   Make 48.

4. Join the units as shown to complete 48 blocks.

 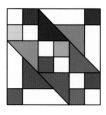

Make 48.

Quilt Assembly and Borders

1. Arrange the blocks as shown in the quilt assembly diagram below. Play with the position of the blocks until you are happy with the color arrangement. Sew the blocks into rows and sew the rows together.

2. Use the 4½" multicolored strips to add the border to the quilt top. The quilt shown has mitered borders; refer to page 20 to attach your borders using whatever method you prefer.

Quilt assembly

Finishing Up

1. Mark quilting lines, if desired.

2. Layer the quilt top with the batting and backing. Baste.

3. Hand or machine quilt. Follow the quilting suggestions shown below or use your own design.

4. Refer to "Binding" on page 23 to bind the quilt.

5. Sign and date your quilt.

TIP To make a quilt with an even scrappier look, use two different cream fabrics or a variety of scraps. You'll need 3 yards for the crosses and 1½ yards for the chain of squares.

ALL THE SPIRIT, HALF THE WORK

It's easy to keep your spirits up while piecing a lap-quilt version of "Summer Spirit"! You'll need about 2⅜ yards of cream fabric, 2⅝ yards of medium and dark scraps, and 1⅛ yards for the border. You'll need slightly less binding fabric (⅝ yard) and only 5 yards of backing to complete this project.

BLOCK SIZE	BORDER	NUMBER OF BLOCKS	BLOCK LAYOUT	QUILT SIZE
12" (same as sample quilt)	Cut 7 strips, 4½" x 42"	24	4 blocks x 6 blocks	56½" x 80½"

another mosaic

By Gayle Bong

THIS IS AN OLD BLOCK done in 1800s reproduction prints, but the construction is thoroughly modern. I've updated the instructions to incorporate folded corners and sandwich-pieced triangles that I call Twin Peaks. Try making this pattern with 1930s-inspired prints, perhaps with solid-colored pinwheels, to put a different spin on this classic look.

Finished quilt: 44½" x 60½"
Finished blocks: 8"

Materials

Yardages are based on 42"-wide fabric.

- 2⅝ yards of cream for background

- 2¼ yards *total* of assorted medium and dark scraps for pinwheels and trapezoids

- 3 yards for backing

- ½ yard for binding

- 50" x 66" piece of batting

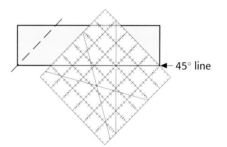

45° line

Cutting

Please read all the directions before starting.

FABRIC	FIRST CUT	FOLLOWING CUTS
Cream	6 strips, 2⅞" x 42"	Cut each strip in half to yield 12 strips, 2⅞" x 21"
	9 strips, 2½" x 42"	140 squares, 2½" x 2½"
	5 strips, 5¼" x 42"	35 squares, 5¼" x 5¼"; cut *each* square in half twice diagonally to yield 140 triangles
	7 strips, 2½" x 42"	20 rectangles, 2½" x 9¼"* 8 rectangles, 2½" x 7¼"*
Medium and Dark Scraps	12 strips, 2⅞" x 19"	
	70 squares, 4⅞" x 4⅞"	Cut *each* square in half once diagonally to yield 140 triangles
	24 squares, 2⅞" x 2⅞"	Cut *each* square in half once diagonally to yield 48 triangles
Binding	6 strips, 2¼" x 42"	

Trim a 45° triangle from each end of the cream rectangles to make trapezoids. (See above.)

Making the Blocks

1. Place a 2⅞" x 19" medium or dark strip on top of a 2⅞" x 21" cream strip with right sides together. Sew the strips together along *both* long edges as shown. Press to set the seams. Repeat to make 12 strip sets. Cut the strip sets into 70 squares, 2⅞" each. Cut each square in half once diagonally to yield 140 Twin Peaks units. Cut all the strip sets with the dark fabric on top and be sure to cut all diagonals in the same direction as shown. Press toward the darker fabric.

2⅞"

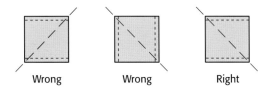

Make 12 strip sets.
Cut 70 segments.

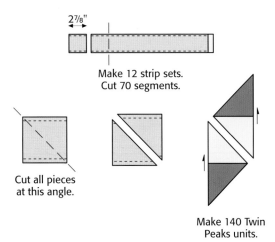

Cut all pieces
at this angle.

Make 140 Twin
Peaks units.

TIP There are a couple of ways to cut these pieces incorrectly, but only one way to cut them correctly. Make sure your piece placement matches the diagram *before* you cut through the corners of the square!

Wrong   Wrong   Right

2. Sew a cream 5¼" triangle to a Twin Peaks unit as shown. Repeat to make 140 triangle units.

Make 140.

3. Referring to "Folded Corners" on page 16, sew a cream 2½" square to a 4⅞" medium or dark triangle. Press and trim the excess. Repeat to make 140 units.

Make 140.

4. Sew the units from steps 2 and 3 together. Press the seam allowances toward the folded-corner unit.

5. Join four units with identical pinwheel triangles into pairs, and sew the pairs into a block. Before pressing, undo two stitches in the seam allowance at the center of the block. This will let the seams fall open in a pinwheel fashion, which will help to distribute the bulk at the center of the block. Press as shown. Repeat to make 35 blocks.

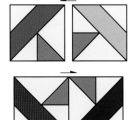
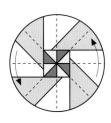

Press the seam
allowance open.

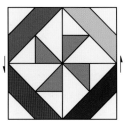

Make 35.

Quilt Assembly and Borders

1. Arrange the blocks as shown in the quilt assembly diagram at right. When you are happy with the color arrangement, sew the blocks into rows and then sew the rows together. Press.

2. Sew a 2⅞" medium or dark triangle to each end of a 9¼" trapezoid. Press the seam allowances in one direction. Repeat to make 20 units.

Make 20.

3. Sew a 2⅞" medium or dark triangle to one end of a 7¼" trapezoid. Repeat to make four units with the triangle on the right side and four with the triangle on the left.

Make 4.   Make 4.

4. Join the trapezoid units to make four borders as shown. Begin and end each border with one of the end units made in step 3.

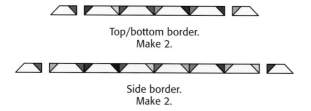

Top/bottom border.
Make 2.

Side border.
Make 2.

5. Pin the border strips to the quilt, matching centers, quarter points, and ends. Sew the borders to the quilt, easing to fit, and begin and end your stitching ¼" from each corner. (This will allow for the mitered seam at the corner.) Backstitch to secure the seams. Sew the diagonal seam in the corner, keeping the seam allowance free. Press.

6. Sew a line of stay stitching 3⁄16" from the edge of the quilt. This will prevent the seams in the pieced border from coming loose around the edge of the quilt.

Quilt assembly

Finishing Up

1. Mark quilting lines, if desired.

2. Layer the quilt top with the batting and backing. Baste.

3. Hand or machine quilt. Follow the quilting suggestions shown below or use your own design.

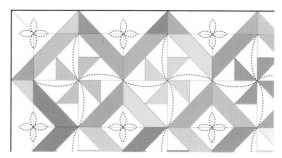

4. Refer to "Binding" on page 23 to bind the quilt.

5. Sign and date your quilt.

spring break

By Gayle Bong

T HE DEEP, RICH PRINTS in this quilt are brightened by the cotton-candy pink background, proving that the background doesn't always have to be light beige! These square-in-a-square blocks, with four-patch units in the center and sandwich-pieced triangles, are easy to construct, and the unusual sashing treatment adds interest to an already sparkling quilt.

Finished quilt: 64" x 72½"
Finished blocks: 8½"

Materials

Yardages are based on 42"-wide fabric.

- 2⅜ yards of light pink for outer border and binding
- 1½ yards *total* of assorted light pink scraps for blocks
- 1½ yards *total* of assorted medium and dark scraps for blocks
- 1 yard of medium teal for sashing
- ½ yard *total* of assorted cream scraps for blocks
- 4 yards for backing
- 70" x 78" piece of batting

Cutting
Please read all the directions before starting.

FABRIC	FIRST CUT	FOLLOWING CUTS
Medium and Dark Scraps	14 strips, 2" x 21"	
	21 strips, 3" x 21"	
Cream	60 squares, 3" x 3"	Cut *each* square in half once diagonally to yield 120 triangles
Light Pink Scraps	9 strips, 5⅛" x 42"	60 squares, 5⅛" x 5⅛"; cut *each* square in half once diagonally to yield 120 triangles
	4 squares, 2¼" x 2¼"	
Medium Teal	11 strips, 2¼" x 42"	2 strips, 2¼" x 34½"
		2 strips, 2¼" x 26"
		8 strips, 2¼" x 9"
Light Pink	8 strips, 7½" x 42"	
	7 strips, 2¼" x 42"	

Making the Blocks

1. Sew all the 2" x 21" medium and dark strips together into one long strip set, staggering the ends by 10". There's no need to sew the strips together by their short ends before making the set. Just start sewing two strips together along their long edges, and when you reach the end of a strip, simply butt another up to it, whether it is on the top or bottom. Make sure you position pieces right sides together. Press the seam allowance in either direction.

   Cut the strip set into 60 segments, each 2", trimming and discarding any segment that spans the butted ends. Sew the two-square segments together to make 30 four-patch units.

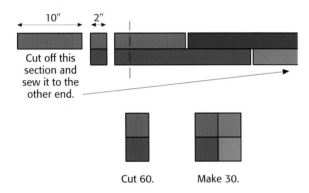

Cut 60.   Make 30.

2. Sew the long edges of two 3" cream triangles to opposite sides of a four-patch unit. Press toward the triangles. Sew cream triangles to the other two sides and press. Repeat to make 30 units.

Match the triangle point with the seams.

Make 30.

> **TIP** Use the center seam of the four-patch unit as a guide to correctly align the triangles for sewing. The tip of the triangle should fall directly on the seam.

3. Place two 3" x 21" medium or dark strips on top of one another with right sides together and ends staggered by about 10". (This will give you a greater number of print combinations.) Sew the strips together *along both long edges*, adding additional strips in the same way you did in step 1. Press the resulting strip to set the seams. Cut 60 squares, 3" each, trimming off and discarding any segment that spans a seam. Cut each square in half once diagonally, alternating the direction of the diagonal cuts as shown. Press the seam allowances open. Make 120 Twin Peaks units.

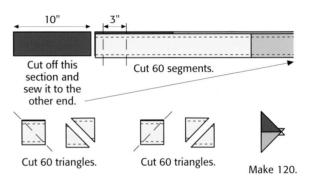

Cut off this section and sew it to the other end.   Cut 60 segments.

Cut 60 triangles.   Cut 60 triangles.   Make 120.

4. Match the tip of an on-point square (from step 2) with the center seam of a Twin Peaks unit and sew them together. Press. Sew a Twin Peaks unit to the opposite side and press. Sew two units to the remaining two sides of the block and press. Repeat to make 30.

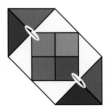 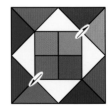

Make 30.

5. Sew a 5⅛" light pink triangle to one side of a unit from step 4, matching the point of the triangle to the seam of the four patch. Repeat on the opposite side. Press the seam allowance toward the light pink triangles. Add triangles to the remaining two sides to

complete the block. Repeat to make 30 blocks.

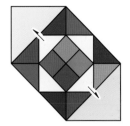 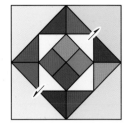

Make 30.

Assembling the Quilt

1. Make five vertical rows of four blocks each. Sew the 2¼" x 34½" teal strips between the first and second rows and the fourth and fifth rows.

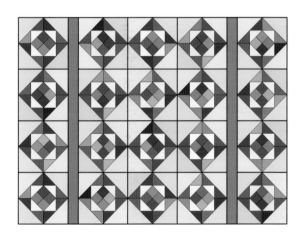

2. Sew two 2¼" x 9" teal strips, two 2¼" light pink squares, and a 2¼" x 26" teal strip together as shown. Repeat to make a second strip. Add them to the top and bottom of quilt.

Make 2.

3. Sew together five blocks and two 2¼" x 9" teal strips as shown. Repeat to make a second row. Sew the rows to the top and bottom of the quilt.

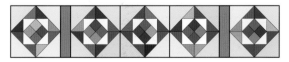

Make 2.

4. Use the remaining 2¼" teal strips to add the inner border to the quilt top. Use the 7½" light pink strips to add the outer border. The quilt shown has straight-cut borders; refer to page 20 to attach your borders using whatever method you prefer.

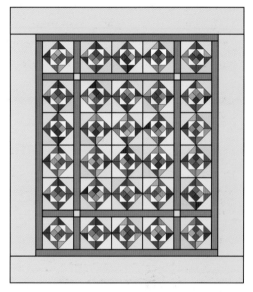

Quilt assembly

Finishing Up

1. Mark quilting lines, if desired.

2. Layer the quilt top with the batting and backing. Baste.

3. Hand or machine quilt. Follow the quilting suggestions shown below or use your own design.

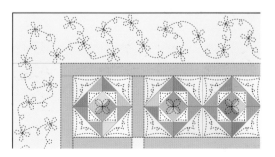

4. Refer to "Binding" on page 23 to bind the quilt.

5. Sign and date your quilt.

crossed tracks

By Gayle Bong—quilted by Carol Gunderson

I WAS SURPRISED to find that the gold accent squares are actually my favorite part of this quilt. Any color could be used, as long as it matches your bar units. If gold isn't your thing, choose your favorite color or try out different colors from your 3½" scrap box after the bar units are constructed. Choose the light background and final border last.

Finished quilt: 88" x 101"

Finished plain squares: 6" • Finished bar units: 3" x 6"

Materials

Yardages are based on 42"-wide fabric.

For the quilt:

- 2¼ yards *total* of assorted medium and dark scraps for bar units
- 2¼ yards of cream for background
- ⅝ yard of gold for accent squares
- 9 yards for backing
- 95" x 107" piece of batting

For the borders and binding:

- 2 yards of brown for outer border
- 1⅜ yards of gold for inner borders
- ⅞ yard of cream for background
- 66 assorted dark 3½" x 3½" squares for on-point border squares
- ⅞ yard for binding

Cutting

Please read all the directions before starting.

FABRIC	FIRST CUT	FOLLOWING CUTS
Cream for Quilt Center Background	2 strips, 15" x 42"	4 squares, 15" x 15"; cut *each* square in half twice diagonally to yield 16 triangles (you will use 14)
		2 squares, 10" x 10"; cut *each* square in half once diagonally to yield 4 triangles.
	6 strips, 6½" x 42"	32 squares, 6½" x 6½"
Gold for Accent Squares	5 strips, 3½" x 42"	49 squares, 3½" x 3½"
Medium and Dark Scraps for Bar Units	42 strips, 1½" x 42"	
Cream for Border Background	5 strips, 5¼" x 42"	33 squares, 5¼" x 5¼"; cut *each* square in half twice diagonally to yield 132 triangles
Gold for Inner Borders	7 strips, 2¼" x 42"	
	8 strips, 3¼" x 42"	
Brown for Outer Border	6 lengthwise-cut strips, 6½"	
Binding	10 strips, 2¼" x 42"	

Making the Quilt Center

1. Cut the 1½" medium and dark strips in half so they're about 21" long. Sew them together in sets of three strips, combining the colors so you have many different combinations. Press the seams in either direction. Sew the sets into one long strip set, staggering the ends of the strips by about 10" as shown. Press. Remove the three-strip tail from the beginning of the set and attach it to the end of the set so all segments are six strips wide. (Strip sets should measure 6½" wide.) Cutting through all six strips, cut 80 segments, each 3½" wide. These are the bar units.

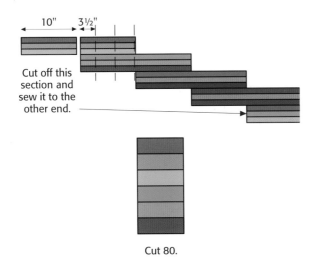

Cut 80.

TIP Press from the right side of the strip set after adding each strip. This will make it easier to avoid tucks along the seam lines. After pressing, check the back for flat seam allowances.

2. Lay out the bar units, gold accent squares, and cream squares in rows as shown. Add the fourteen 15" cream triangles as setting triangles and the four 10" cream triangles as corner triangles. When you're happy with the color placement, sew together the rows of bar units and accent squares, pressing toward the squares. Next sew together the rows of bar units and cream squares,

pressing toward the squares. (Follow the illustration for the number of units per row and correct placement of the setting triangles.) Refer to "Diagonal Quilt Assembly" on page 19 and sew the rows together, pressing toward the large squares. Square up the edges of the quilt top to 56½" x 69¼".

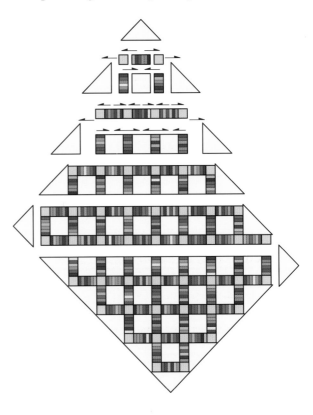

Making the Borders

1. Sew cream triangles to two adjacent sides of a medium or dark 3½" square. Repeat to make 64 units. Sew cream triangles to two opposite sides of a medium or dark 3½" square as shown. Repeat to make two of these end units for the side borders.

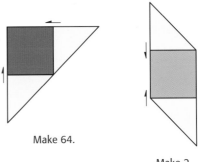

Make 64.

Make 2.

2. Join 15 units to make the top border. Repeat to make the bottom border. Join 17 units to make a side border, adding one end unit from step 1 last. Repeat to make a second side border.

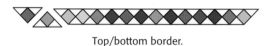

Top/bottom border.
Make 2.

Side border.
Make 2.

3. Using the 2¼" gold strips, add the inner border to the quilt top referring to "Straight-Cut Borders" on page 20.

4. Pin all four pieced border strips to the quilt, matching centers, quarter points, and ends. Sew the borders to the quilt, easing where necessary. Miter the corners.

5. Using the 3¼" gold strips and the 6½" brown strips, add the final borders to the quilt top as shown.

Quilt assembly

Finishing Up

1. Mark quilting lines, if desired.

2. Layer the quilt top with the batting and backing. Baste.

3. Hand or machine quilt. Follow the quilting suggestions shown below or use your own design.

4. Refer to "Binding" on page 23 to bind the quilt.

5. Sign and date your quilt.

brickwork

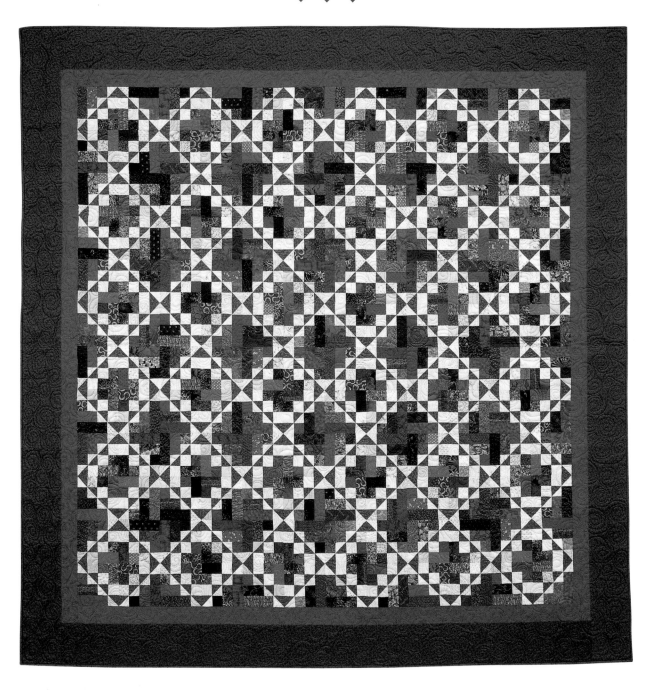

By Gayle Bong

T HE SHADED FOUR-PATCH technique known as Mary's Triangles is expanded here to use four different strip sets to make a shaded 16-patch unit! Choose the majority of your scraps from one side of the color wheel and choose just one accent color from the opposite side for a truly eye-catching quilt.

Finished quilt: 89½" x 89½"
Finished blocks: 12"

Materials

Yardages are based on 42"-wide fabric.

- 4 yards of assorted medium and dark prints
- 3 yards *total* of light scraps for background
- 2 yards of brown for outer border
- 1⅝ yards of blue for complementary triangles
- ⅞ yard of brick red for inner border
- 8½ yards for backing
- ¾ yard for binding
- 95" x 95" piece of batting

Cutting

Please read all the directions before starting.

FABRIC	CUT
Blue	16 strips, 3¼" x 42"
Light Scraps	16 strips, 3¼" x 42"
	24 strips, 2" x 42"
Medium and Dark Prints	32 strips, 2" x 21"
	32 strips, 3½" x 21"
	16 strips, 5" x 21"
Brick Red	8 strips, 3" x 42"
Brown	9 strips, 6½" x 42"
Binding	10 strips, 2¼" x 42"

Making the Blocks

Accurate seam allowances are very important to the success of this quilt. Review "The Quilter's Quarter Inch" on page 17 before beginning.

1. Crosscut all the blue and the light strips in half so each strip is at least 20" long. Sew blue, light, and medium or dark strips together as shown to make two different strip sets. Make 16 of each set, pressing the seam allowances as indicated by the arrows. The strip sets should measure 7¾" wide. Cut each strip set into 144 segments, each 2" wide.

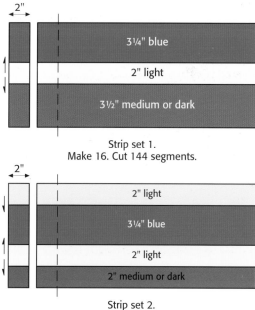

Strip set 1.
Make 16. Cut 144 segments.

Strip set 2.
Make 16. Cut 144 segments.

2. Sew the units into 144 pairs *exactly* as shown. Turn one sewn pair 180° and sew it to another pair to make a block. Flip the block over and clip the seam allowances to the seam line where the blue pieces meet so that you can press as shown. Blocks should measure 6½" x 7¾". Repeat to make 72 blocks.

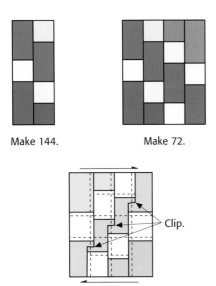

Make 144.   Make 72.

3. Sew light and medium or dark strips together as shown to make two more strip sets. Make 16 of each set, pressing the seam allowances as indicated by the arrows. The strip sets should measure 7¾" wide. Cut each strip set into 144 segments, each 2" wide.

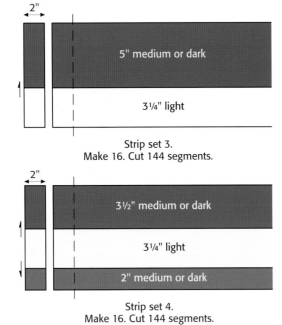

2"

5" medium or dark

3¼" light

Strip set 3.
Make 16. Cut 144 segments.

2"

3½" medium or dark

3¼" light

2" medium or dark

Strip set 4.
Make 16. Cut 144 segments.

4. Repeat step 2 with the 2" units from strip sets 3 and 4. Carefully sew them together in pairs *exactly* as shown. Rotate one pair 180° and sew it to another pair to make a block. Flip the block over and clip the seam allowances to the seam line where the light pieces meet so that you can press as shown. Repeat to make 72 blocks.

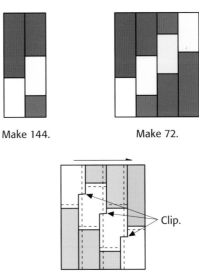

Make 144.   Make 72.

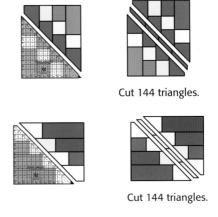

5. Cut two triangles from each of the blocks made in steps 2 and 4. If you're using a triangle rotary ruler, measure a 6⅞" triangle as shown; cut on the diagonal. Be careful to allow a ¼" seam allowance past the corners of the triangles. Rotate the remaining piece, measure, and cut again. There will be a little bit of waste between the units and a tip of each unit will be missing, but the seam allowance is large enough that this doesn't pose a problem.

Cut 144 triangles.

Cut 144 triangles.

If you don't have a triangle rotary ruler, you can substitute a standard ruler. Follow the directions in step 5 on page 52, cutting your triangle template from a 6⅞" square.

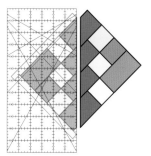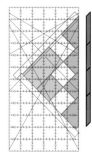

Butt tape against block.

6. Sew a blue-edged triangle and a light-edged triangle together to make a quarter block. Repeat to make 144 quarter blocks. Join four quarters as shown to complete 36 blocks.

Make 144.

Make 36.

Assembling the Quilt

1. Lay out the blocks in six rows of six blocks each as shown in the quilt assembly diagram at upper right. When you are happy with the color arrangement, sew the blocks into rows and then sew the rows together.

2. Using the 3" brick red strips, sew the inner border to the quilt top. The quilt shown

has straight-cut borders; refer to page 20 to attach your borders using whatever method you prefer. Use the 6½" brown strips to attach the outer border.

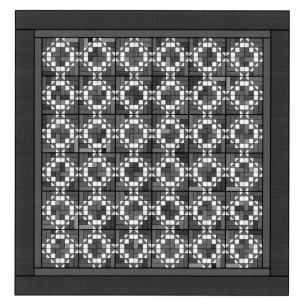

Quilt assembly

Finishing Up

1. Mark quilting lines, if desired.

2. Layer the quilt top with the batting and backing. Baste.

3. Hand or machine quilt. Follow the quilting suggestions shown below or use your own design.

4. Refer to "Binding" on page 23 to bind the quilt.

5. Sign and date your quilt.

A FEW BRICKS SHORT

If your scrap stash isn't quite bulging with suitable candidates for this quilt, you might try making a smaller version. Yardage requirements are listed below for two great alternatives to the full-size quilt.

SIZE	BLOCK SIZE	NUMBER OF 21" STRIP SETS	NUMBER OF 2" SEGMENTS TO CUT FROM EACH SET	NUMBER OF BLOCKS	BLOCK LAYOUT
Lap (65½" x 77½")	12" (same as sample quilt)	8 each of sets 1, 2, 3, and 4	80	20	4 x 5
Twin (77½" x 89½")	12" (same as sample quilt)	12 each of sets 1, 2, 3, and 4	120	30	5 x 6

Materials

Yardages are based on 42"-wide fabric.

	LAP	TWIN
Blue for the Complementary Triangles	⅞ yard	1¼ yards
Assorted Medium and Dark Prints for Blocks	2 yards	2½ yards
Light Scraps for Background	1⅝ yards	2⅜ yards
Inner Border	⅝ yard	¾ yard
Outer Border	1½ yards	1⅞ yards
Backing	4 yards	5¼ yards
Binding	⅝ yard	¾ yard
Batting	70" x 82"	85" x 97"

potluck

By Gayle Bong

W HEN I LOOKED at my black-and-white sketch of this quilt, I realized the pattern would be perfect for the 1800s reproduction prints I'm so fond of. To give your quilt the same unified look I've given this one, choose a theme and select your print combinations accordingly. No matter what fabrics you choose, though, you'll have fun strip piecing the three-patch triangles. And the alternate plain triangles give you ample room to show off a pretty quilting design, be it traditional or contemporary.

Finished quilt: 82½" x 84½"
Finished blocks: 12"

Materials

Yardages are based on 42"-wide fabric.

- 4¾ yards of medium light pink for plain triangles and border

- 1⅜ yards *total* of assorted dark prints for blocks

- 1⅜ yards *total* of assorted medium prints for blocks

- 1⅝ yards *total* of assorted light prints for blocks

- 7½ yards for backing

- ⅝ yard for binding

- 88" x 90" piece of batting

Cutting

Please read all the directions before starting. Once all the strips are cut, the Clearview Triangle Ruler is used for all other cutting. See "Working with 60° Angles" on page 13.

FABRIC	FIRST CUT	ADDITIONAL CUTS
Assorted Light Prints	14 strips, 3¼" x 42"	Cut in half to yield 28 strips, each 3¼" x 21" (You'll use 27.)
	6 strips, 2¾" x 12"	From *each* strip, cut 6 equilateral (60°) triangles (36 total)
Assorted Dark Prints	27 strips, 2½" x 20"	
	6 strips, 2½" x 14"	From *each* strip, cut 4 diamonds, 2½" (24 total)
Assorted Medium Prints	27 strips, 4¾" x 12"	From *each* strip, cut 3 equilateral (60°) triangles, 4¾" (81 total)
Medium Light Pink	7 strips, 12¾" x 42"	27 equilateral (60°) triangles, 12¾"
	1 strip, 13¼" x 42"	4 rectangles, 7⅝" x 13¼"; with wrong sides together, cut pairs of rectangles in half once diagonally to yield 8 triangles. You will use 6.
	8 strips, 6½" x 42"	
Binding	9 strips, 2¼" x 42"	

Additional Cutting

From each of the 6 different medium scraps, cut:

- 1 equilateral (60°) triangle, 4¾" tall
- 1 matching rectangle, 5¼" x 3⅛"

Cut 3 of the rectangles in half diagonally in one direction and cut 3 rectangles diagonally in the opposite direction to make reverse half triangles. You'll use 1 triangle of each color.

Making the Blocks

For each block, choose a set of three fabrics—a light, a medium, and a dark print. As you cut and sew patches, keep the colors together so you can be sure you have all the matching pieces you need for each block.

1. Sew a 2½" dark strip to a 3¼" light strip. Repeat to make 27 sets. Cut 2½" segments at a 60° angle. (See "Working with 60° Angles" on page 13.) Cut 6 segments from each set for 162 segments total.

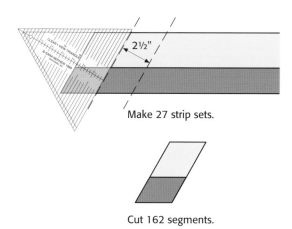

Make 27 strip sets.

Cut 162 segments.

2. Sew two segments together as shown to make a diamond-shaped four-patch unit. Note that the seams do not meet in the center. Turn the piece over and clip the seam allowance in the center of the seam.

Press each end of the seam allowance toward the light fabric. Make 81 uneven four-patch units.

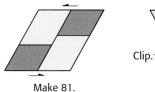

Clip.

Make 81.

3. Measure and cut a 4¾"-tall three-patch triangle unit from a four-patch unit. Turn the remaining piece, measure, and trim a second three-patch triangle. There will be a little bit of waste between the units, and a tip of each unit will be missing, but the seam allowance is large enough that it won't pose a problem. Repeat to cut 162 triangle units.

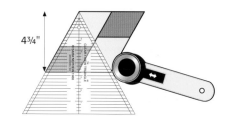

4¾"

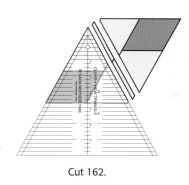

Cut 162.

4. Sew a triangle unit to a medium print 4¾" triangle to form a diamond-shaped unit. You'll need three of each color combination for a total of 81 units.

Make 3 of each color combination (81 total).

5. Sew two triangle units from step 3 to adjacent sides of a diamond unit from step 4.

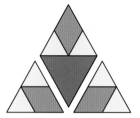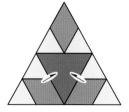

Make 1 of each
color combination.

6. Sew diamond units to two adjacent sides of a triangle unit.

Make 1 of each
color combination.

7. Join the top and bottom sections to complete a block. Press the seam allowances toward the two larger triangles. Repeat to make 27 blocks.

Make 27.

Making the Half Blocks

You will need three half blocks and three reversed half blocks for the sides of the quilt. Use a different set of fabrics for each.

1. Sew a light print 2¾" triangle to a dark print diamond. Finger-press the seam allowance toward the diamond. Sew another light print triangle to the adjacent side of the diamond to make a triangle unit. Repeat to make a matching triangle unit. Repeat to make six sets of two matching units, using a different set of fabrics for each half block (12 total).

Make 2 for
each half block
(12 total).

2. Sew a medium 4¾" triangle to one of the units from step 1 to make a diamond unit. Repeat to make six total.

Make 1 for each
half block (6 total).

3. Bisect the remaining dark diamonds, cutting ¼" past the center points as shown. Discard the smaller pieces or put them in your scrap stash.

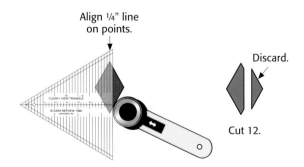

Align ¼" line
on points.

Discard.

Cut 12.

4. Sew a light print triangle to a dark print half diamond, forming a half triangle. Make two of these units for each half block; then sew one of them to a medium print half triangle that you cut from your matching rectangles. *Note:* You will only use half of these cut triangles, and you will need to use mirror image triangles for the left and right side half blocks.

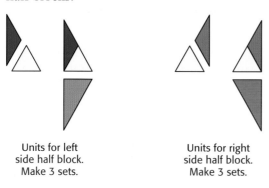

Units for left
side half block.
Make 3 sets.

Units for right
side half block.
Make 3 sets.

5. Join the units as shown to complete the half block. Repeat to make six half blocks.

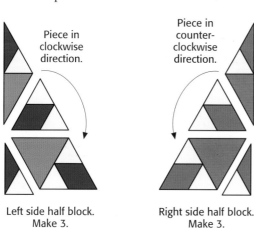

Piece in
clockwise
direction.

Piece in
counter-
clockwise
direction.

Left side half block.
Make 3.

Right side half block.
Make 3.

Assembling the Quilt

1. Arrange the 12¾" pink alternate blocks, the pieced blocks, and the half blocks as shown in the quilt assembly diagram at upper right. Add the pink 13¼" triangles to the outer edges to square up the quilt. When you're happy with the color arrangement, sew the blocks into rows, pressing the seam allowances toward the plain blocks in each row. Sew the rows together.

2. Using the 6½" pink strips, add the border to the quilt top, referring to the directions for "Straight-Cut Borders" on page 20.

Quilt assembly

Finishing Up

1. Mark quilting lines, if desired.

2. Layer the quilt top with the batting and backing. Baste.

3. Hand or machine quilt. Follow the quilting suggestions shown below or use your own design.

4. Refer to "Binding" on page 23 to bind the quilt.

5. Sign and date your quilt.

fractured diamonds

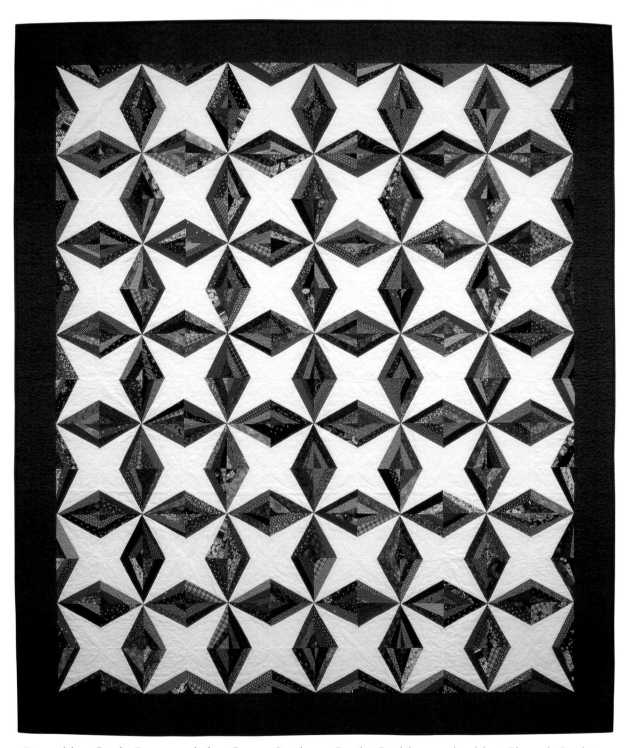

Pieced by Gayle Bong and the Crazy Quilters Quilt Guild—quilted by Cheryl Gerbing

THIS POPULAR DESIGN uses scraps of varying widths sewn to a fabric foundation that stays in place and shows through as the light four-pointed star. Medium and dark scraps in any and all colors can be used, or you can limit yourself to just one color, as we did. The blocks in the quilt shown are 13" finished, but the pattern has been adjusted to make better use of the fabric and has 12" finished blocks.

Finished quilt: 84½" x 96½"
Finished blocks: 12"

Materials

Yardages are based on 42"-wide fabric.

- 6 yards *total* of assorted medium and dark scraps for pieced diamonds

- 5½ yards of white for foundation and star points

- 3 yards of blue print for border

- 7¾ yards for backing

- ¾ yard for binding

- 90" x 102" piece of batting

Making the Blocks

1. Use a pencil and ruler to mark placement lines for the strips on the right side of each white square. To do this, mark a dot where the ¼" seam lines meet in one corner. Align the ¼" line of the ruler on the dot you've just marked and the 3" line of the ruler on the opposite corner and draw a line. Repeat on the adjacent side of the square as shown. Mark all 168 squares this way.

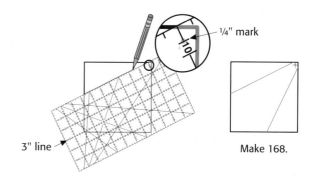

¼" mark

3" line

Make 168.

Cutting
Please read all the directions before starting.

FABRIC	FIRST CUT	FOLLOWING CUTS
White	28 strips, 6½" x 42"	168 squares, 6½" x 6½"
Medium and Dark Scraps	Scraps 1" to 2" wide and 3" or longer	
Blue Print	4 lengthwise-cut strips, 6½" x 100"	
Binding	10 strips, 2¼" x 42"	

You could make a template to mark the placement lines on the blocks. Cut a 6½" square of template material and draw the lines as directed in step 1. Cut away the triangles on opposite sides of the square and use the remaining kite-shaped piece to mark your lines.

2. With right sides together, place the raw edge of a medium or dark scrap on the marked line as shown. (The bulk of the strip should fall toward the middle of the square.) Make sure both ends of the scrap extend past the foundation. Stitch ¼" from the raw edge of the strip. Flip the strip to the right side, covering the line you marked, and press. Trim both ends of the strip even with the foundation.

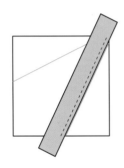 

To save time, trim by making a rough cut with scissors and then trim all the strips perfectly even with the foundation after the square is completed in step 4.

3. Place the next strip at a *slight* angle to the first strip, again making sure the ends of the scrap extend past the foundation. Sew, flip, press, and trim. Repeat with at least one more strip, or until the side of the foundation is covered.

4. Repeat steps 2 and 3 on the other line marked on the foundation. Arrange the strips to be nearly parallel, placing the end of the second and third strip a bit closer to the point where the strips meet. The seams of the first strips will overlap in the corner. This point where they meet will show you the exact ¼" seam allowance needed to create crisp star points when the blocks are sewn together. Repeat with all 168 foundations. Trim all the squares even with the foundation if you have not already done so.

Right.   Wrong.

Slant strips with the narrow ends near the white point, not with the wide ends near the white point.

5. Align the raw edges of four foundation squares as shown to make a star. Join the squares into pairs and then join the pairs to complete the block. Make 42 blocks.

   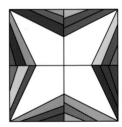

Make 42.

Assembling the Quilt

1. Arrange the blocks as shown in the quilt assembly diagram below. When you are happy with the color arrangement, sew the blocks into rows. Then sew the rows together.

2. Use the 6½" blue print strips to sew the border to the quilt top. The quilt shown has mitered borders; refer to page 20 to attach your borders using whatever method you prefer.

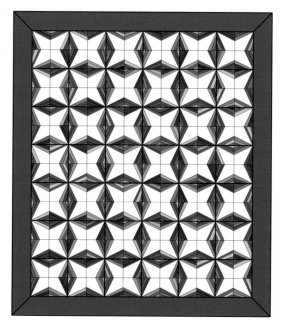

Quilt assembly

Finishing Up

1. Mark quilting lines, if desired.

2. Layer the quilt top with the batting and backing. Baste.

3. Hand or machine quilt. Follow the quilting suggestions shown below or use your own design.

4. Refer to "Binding" on page 23 to bind the quilt.

5. Sign and date your quilt.

everyday dishes

By Gayle Bong

I N THIS QUILT, the focus fabric used for the border determined the color of the scraps used in the quilt. You can make the dark diamonds match in each block, as mine do, or you can join them randomly. For a more casual look, try combining different pairs of scraps for each block.

Finished quilt: 61½" x 75½"
Finished blocks: 12"

Materials

Yardages are based on 42"-wide fabric.

- 3 yards of multicolored print for borders, blocks, and binding

- 3 yards of light gold for background

- ⅞ yard *total* of assorted medium and dark scraps for blocks

- ⅝ yard of light green or dark gold for blocks and inner border

- 3¾ yards for backing

- 67" x 81" piece of batting

Cutting

Please read all the directions before starting. Once all the strips are cut, the Clearview Triangle Ruler is used for all the 60° cutting. See "Working with 60° Angles" on page 13.

FABRIC	FIRST CUT	FOLLOWING CUTS
Medium and Dark Scraps	10 strips, 2½" x 42"	
Light Gold	13 strips, 3¼" x 42"	
	3 strips, 2¾" x 42"	60 equilateral (60°) triangles
	2 strips, 6¾" x 42"	18 equilateral (60°) triangles
	1 strip, 11¼" x 42"	2 rectangles, 11¼" x 19¼"*
	3 strips, 3½" x 42"	
Light Green or Dark Gold	3 strips, 2½" x 42"	30 diamonds, 2½" x 2½"**
	7 strips, 1½" x 42"	
Multicolored Print	3 strips, 2½" x 42"	
	5 strips, 2½" x 42"	30 parallelograms, 2½" x 4½"
	4 strips, 4¾" x 42"	38 equilateral (60°) triangles
	2 strips, 4¾" x 42"	8 rectangles, 4½" x 8"
	7 strips, 5" x 42"	
	7 strips, 2¼" x 42"	

*With wrong sides together, cut the rectangles in half once diagonally to yield 4 corner setting triangles.
**To make a quilt like the one shown on page 84, cut 15 light green diamonds and 15 dark gold diamonds.

Making the Blocks

1. Cut three diamonds from each of the 2½" medium and dark strips for a total of 30 diamonds. Sew the remainder of one of the 2½" medium or dark strips to a 3¼" light gold strip. Repeat to make 10 sets. Cut a total of 72 segments, each 2½" wide, at a 60° angle as shown. (See "Working with 60° Angles" on page 13 for more information.)

Cut 3 diamonds from each medium and dark strip (30 total).

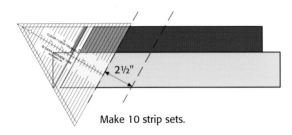

Make 10 strip sets.

Cut 72 segments.

2. Turn one segment 180° and sew it to a matching segment to make an uneven four-patch unit. Note that the seams do not meet in the center. Turn the piece over and clip the seam allowance in the center of the seam. Press each end of the seam allowance toward the light gold fabric. Repeat to make 36 four-patch units.

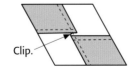

Make 36.

Clip.

3. Measure and cut a 4¾"-tall three-patch triangle from a four-patch unit. Turn the remaining piece, measure, and trim a second three-patch triangle. There is a little bit of waste between the units, and a tip of each unit will be missing, but the seam allowance is large enough that this doesn't pose a problem. Repeat to cut 72 triangle units.

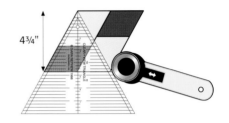

4¾"

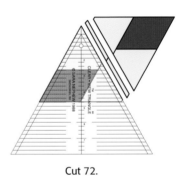

Cut 72.

4. Sew a medium or dark diamond cut in step 1 between a light green or dark gold diamond and a 2¾" light gold triangle. Sew to the unit from step 3. Make 30. Set aside the remaining three-patch triangles for the border.

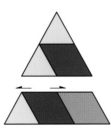
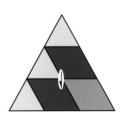

Make 30.

5. Sew a 2½" multicolored strip to a 3¼" light gold strip. Repeat to make three strip sets. Cut a total of 30 segments, each 2½" wide, at a 60° angle.

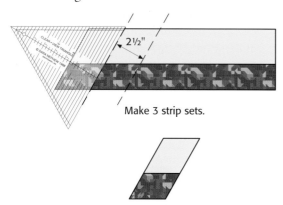

2½"

Make 3 strip sets.

Cut 30 segments.

6. Turn one segment 180° and sew it to a matching segment to make an uneven four-patch unit. Clip the seam allowance in the center of the seam and press each end of the seam allowance toward the dark fabric. Repeat to make 15 four-patch units. Measure and cut a 4¾"-tall three-patch triangle from the four-patch unit as you did in step 3. Turn the remaining piece, measure, and trim a second three-patch triangle. Repeat to cut 30 units.

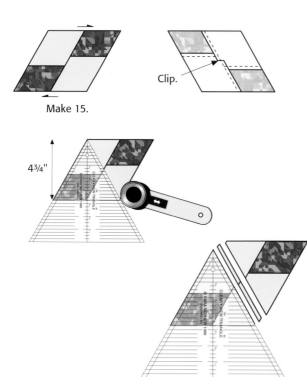

Make 15.

Clip.

4¾"

Cut 30 triangle units.

7. Sew a light gold 2¾" triangle to one end of a multicolored parallelogram. Add this unit to a three-patch triangle cut in step 6. Repeat to make 30 units.

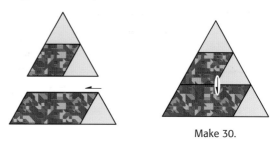

Make 30.

8. Sew the units from steps 4 and 7 together as shown to complete the blocks. Join three units to make each half block; then join the two halves. Repeat to make 10 blocks.

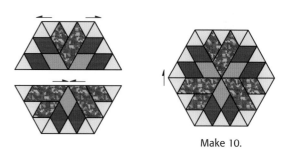

Make 10.

Assembling the Quilt

1. Sew two 6¾" light gold triangles to opposite sides of six blocks to make diamond-shaped blocks. Sew only one light gold triangle to the remaining four blocks.

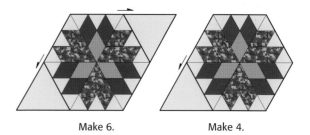

Make 6.   Make 4.

2. Arrange the blocks, the remaining two 6¾" light gold triangles, and the corner triangles as shown. Sew the blocks together into rows. Sew the rows together and then add the large corner triangles.

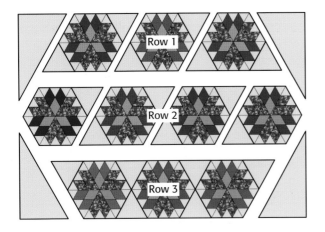

Making the Borders

1. Sew the 3½" light gold strips together end to end. Cut two strips, each 56" long. Sew them to the two long sides of the quilt top, easing to fit if necessary.

2. Join a remaining three-patch triangle unit with a 4¾" multicolored triangle as shown. Repeat to make 38 units.

Make 38.

3. With wrong sides together, cut a 30°-angle piece from one end of each pair of 4½" x 8" multicolored rectangles.

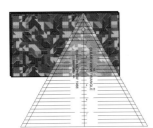
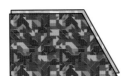

Cut 4 pairs (8 total).

4. Join the units from step 2 to make the pieced borders. For the top and bottom borders, sew eight units together as shown and add a three-patch triangle unit to one end. Begin and end each border with a 4½"-wide trapezoid. (These pieces will provide the extra fabric necessary to miter the corners of the pieced border.) For the side borders, sew 11 units together as shown and add a three-patch triangle to one end and trapezoids to both ends.

Top/bottom border.
Make 2.

Side border.
Make 2.

5. At each end of the four pieced border strips, determine where the miter is to begin on the inner edge—exactly ¼" from the edge—and mark each point with a pin. Draw the 45° miter line on the wrong side of the pieced border, starting at the pin and ending at the outside corner as shown.

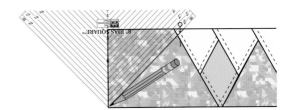

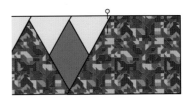

6. Pin all four pieced border strips to the quilt, matching centers, quarter points, and ends. Sew the borders to the quilt, easing to fit if necessary. Avoid stitching into the seam allowance at the corners. Referring to "Mitered Borders" on page 21, miter the corners, sewing on the lines you drew in step 5.

7. Sew the 1½" light green or dark gold strips together end to end. Sew the 5" multicolored strips together end to end. Sew the two strips together along their long edges before adding them to the quilt to make the inner and outer borders. Sew the borders to the quilt top, mitering the corners.

Quilt assembly

Finishing Up

1. Mark quilting lines, if desired.

2. Layer the quilt top with the batting and backing. Baste.

3. Hand or machine quilt. Follow the quilting suggestions shown below or use your own design.

4. Refer to "Binding" on page 23 to bind the quilt.

5. Sign and date your quilt.

shimmer and shine

By Gayle Bong

Don't be fooled by all the diamonds and triangles—this quilt has no set-in seams to deal with, so construction is simple! Just cut split diamonds from a strip-pieced panel and then join them into triangular blocks. You could broaden the range of colors a little to add more shimmer to your stars, or you could use a tight range of color in the star centers and points, as I did. Another option would be to use one color for the star center and a different color for the points.

Finished quilt: 53" x 67½"
Finished block height: 12"

Materials

Yardages are based on 42"-wide fabric.

- 2⅝ yards of cream for background

- 1⅛ yards *total* of assorted medium or dark scraps **(set 1)** for star centers*

- 1⅛ yards of multicolored large-scale print

- ¾ yard *total* of assorted medium or dark scraps **(set 2)** for star points*

- 3¼ yards for backing

- ⅝ yard for binding

- 58" x 73" piece of batting

*To make a quilt like the one on page 90, choose two sets of fabric that are the same color; each fabric should appear either in the star points or in the star centers, but not in both.

Cutting

Please read all the directions before starting. Once all the strips are cut, the Clearview Triangle Ruler is used for all 60° cutting. See "Working with 60° Angles" on page 13.

FABRIC	FIRST CUT	FOLLOWING CUTS
Medium or Dark Scraps (set 2)	9 strips, 2¼" x 42"	
Cream	9 strips, 2¼" x 42"	
	5 strips, 2½" x 42"	60 diamonds, 2½"
	1 strip, 4¾" x 42"	8 equilateral (60°) triangles
	1 strip, 21¼" x 42"	2 rectangles, 12¼" x 21¼"; place rectangles wrong sides together and cut in half once diagonally to yield corner setting triangles
	4 strips, 3½" x 42"	
	6 border strips, 1¾" x 42"	
Medium or Dark Scraps (set 1)	13 strips, 2½" x 42"	164 diamonds, 2½"
Multicolored Large-Scale Print	7 strips, 4¾" x 42"	82 equilateral (60°) triangles
Binding	7 strips, 2¼" x 42"	

Making the Blocks

1. Sew nine pairs of 2¼" cream strips and 2¼" medium or dark strips together. Press the seam allowances toward the dark strips. Then sew four pairs into one panel as shown and five pairs into a second panel. Press toward the dark strips.

Make 1 panel with 8 strips and 1 panel with 10 strips.

TIP Press from the right side of the strip set after adding each strip. This will make it easier to avoid tucks along the seam lines. After pressing, check the back for flat seam allowances.

2. Place the centerline of a Clearview triangle ruler on the first seam as shown and measure 5". Cut on each side of the ruler.

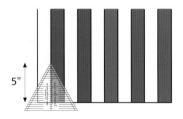

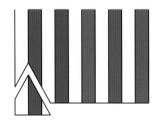

TIP I found that using a small rotary cutter was helpful for this step. It gives you greater control than a large cutter, so you avoid cutting too far into the panel.

3. Turn the piece around and match the seam with the ruler's centerline and again measure 5". Cut again, trimming the excess from the split-diamond unit.

TIP When cut correctly, the split-diamond units and the individual diamonds cut previously should be the same size.

4. Continue cutting split-diamond units, one at a time, in the order shown. Notice that the dark is on the right side of the units cut from the first row (diamonds 1 through 4) and then the dark is on the left in the next row. Rotate and trim each split-diamond unit. (You may find it more efficient to cut all of the diamonds from the panel before turning them around for trimming.) Cut 120 split-diamond units.

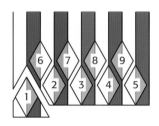

Cut 120.

5. Sew a split-diamond unit to a cream diamond and to a medium or dark diamond as shown below. Sew these units together to make a larger diamond unit. Repeat to make 60 units.

 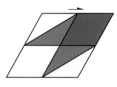

Make 60.

6. Join the large diamond units made in step 5 to the 4¾" multicolored triangles to make the blocks shown in the quantities given. Use the 4¾" cream equilateral triangles in block C.

Block A.
Make 14.

Block B.
Make 10.

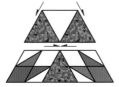 

Block C.
Make 8.

Quilt Assembly and Borders

1. Join the blocks together in four lengthwise rows as shown. Sew the rows together and then add the four large corner triangles, matching the 60° corner of the edge triangles to the 60° corner of the end block.

Block placement diagram

2. Sew two 3½" cream strips together end to end; repeat for the other two. Trim both strips to 60½". Sew the strips to the long sides of the quilt top, easing to fit if necessary.

3. Sew 23 medium or dark diamonds together end to end to make the top inner border; repeat for the bottom border. Sew 29 medium or dark diamonds together end to end to make a side inner border; repeat for the other side border.

Top/bottom border.
Make 2.

Side border.
Make 2.

4. Fold the pieced borders in half and mark their centers. Measure in both directions and mark 24¼" from the center of each short border. Measure in both directions and mark 30¼" from the center of each long border. Pin the pieced borders to the quilt, matching centers and ends. Sew the borders to the quilt, easing to fit if necessary. Avoid stitching into the seam allowance at the corners, and refer to "Mitered Borders" on page 21.

5. Add the 1¾" cream border strips to the quilt top, referring to the directions for "Mitered Borders."

Quilt assembly

Finishing Up

1. Mark quilting lines, if desired.

2. Layer the quilt top with the batting and backing. Baste.

3. Hand or machine quilt. Follow the quilting suggestions shown below or use your own design.

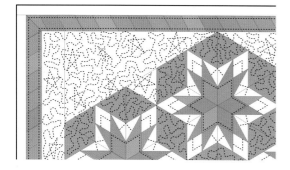

4. Refer to "Binding" on page 23 to bind the quilt.

5. Sign and date your quilt.

FIT FOR A QUEEN

Or to fit a queen—bed, that is. Because one full block and two different partial blocks make up this quilt, it is a little more complicated to enlarge it than some of the others in this book, but the reward is well worth the effort. This quilt will have all of your friends marveling at all those perfectly set-in seams that only you know are pieced in straight rows! Make the border from the multicolored large-scale print rather than pieced diamonds.

Finished queen-size quilt: 83½" x 102½"

Yardages are based on 42"-wide fabric.

4½ yards of cream for background

4⅜ yards of multicolored large-scale print

2⅛ yards *total* of assorted medium or dark scraps (set 2) for star points

1¼ yards *total* of assorted medium or dark scraps (set 1) for star center

8¼ yards for backing

¾ yard for binding

98" x 110" piece of batting

See facing page for Cutting Chart.

Cutting for Queen-Size Shimmer and Shine

Please read all the directions before starting. Once all the strips are cut, the Clearview Triangle Ruler is used for all 60° cutting. See "Working with 60° Angles" on page 13.

FABRIC	FIRST CUT	FOLLOWING CUTS
Medium or Dark Scraps **(set 2)**	30 strips, 2¼" x 42"	
Cream	30 strips, 2¼" x 42"	
	15 strips, 2½" x 42"	192 diamonds, 2½"
	2 strips, 4¾" x 42"	20 equilateral (60°) triangles
	1 strip, 5⅜" x 42"	2 rectangles, 5⅜" x 9¼"; place rectangles wrong sides together and cut in half once diagonally to yield 4 triangles
	2 strips, 7¹¹/₁₆" x 42"	6 rectangles, 7¹¹/₁₆" x 13¼"; place pairs of rectangles wrong sides together and cut in half once diagonally to yield 12 triangles
	4 strips, 3½" x 42"	
Medium or Dark Scraps **(set 1)**	15 strips, 2½" x 42"	192 diamonds, 2½"
Multicolored Large-Scale Print	19 strips, 4¾" x 42"	238 equilateral (60°) triangles
	10 border strips, 4½" x 42"	
Binding	10 strips, 2¼" x 42"	

In general, follow the directions for making the lap-sized quilt. You will need to deviate from those directions as follows:

- When you piece the strip set to cut the split-diamond units in step 1 (page 92), make three panels for easier handling. You'll need to cut 384 split-diamond units.

- You'll need to make 192 of the larger diamond units formed by sewing two split-diamond units to one cream diamond and one medium or dark diamond (step 5, page 92).

- Join the large diamond units to the 4¾" multicolored triangles to make 26 of block A, 42 of block B, and 20 of block C (step 6, page 93).

Lay out the blocks as shown, adding the corner and edge triangles to the ends of the rows before sewing the rows together.

Use the 3½" cream strips to add an inner border to the short ends; then use the 4½" multicolored strips to add the final border to all the edges.

Block placement diagram.
Sew the blocks into 8 rows.

about the author

GAYLE BONG learned to sew by watching her mother. Her first sewing projects were doll clothes, but by ninth grade she was making most of her own clothes. She started quilting in 1981. Designing quilts and writing patterns come naturally to Gayle, who has always been attracted to geometric patterns, fabric, math, puzzles, and writing. She especially loves sharing the excitement of quilting with her students and at guild programs.

Gayle developed unique concepts for designing and cutting quilts and authored books on these concepts. Her first two books, *Infinite Stars* and *Trouble-Free Triangles*, cover the template-free 60° rotary cutting and piecing that she has become known for. In *Thirtysomething* and *Thirtysomething, Too!*, the focus is on easily and accurately working with 30° angles. It's been said that Gayle was "born with a rotary cutter in her hand and a ¼" guide etched into her eyes."

Gayle has the pleasure of spending several hours daily working on her quilts. She lives with her husband, Mark, in Elkhorn, Wisconsin, and she has one grown daughter. In her spare time she enjoys gardening and hiking in the fields and wooded hills around her rural home.